CANCEL

ILLUSTRATED SOURCES IN HISTORY

MUSIC HALL IN BRITAIN

Devastating caricature of Marie Lloyd by Alfred Bryan

MUSIC HALL IN BRITAIN

D. F. CHESHIRE

Rutherford · Madison · Teaneck
Fairleigh Dickinson University Press

First American edition published 1974 by
Associated University Presses, Inc.
Cranbury, New Jersey 08512
Library of Congress Catalogue Card Number: 74-2581
ISBN 0-8386-1563-5
Printed in Great Britain

For Ellen—
so that she can 'remember'
it all as well.

CONTENTS

INTRODUCTION

Music Hall in Britain to 1923—a very big subject, already written about in an ever-increasing number of books, many of which, although useful and entertaining in general, are occasionally misleading, particularly where the development of the genre 'music hall' is concerned. The best comprehensive histories, M. Willson Disher's *Winkles and Champagne* (1938), Raymond Mander and Joe Mitchenson's *British Music Hall* (1965) and Harold Scott's *The Early Doors* (1946), tend to treat the Victorian and Edwardian music hall as though it was a unique form of entertainment rather than the organisation of long-established kinds of performance and performer for financial gain by parties other than the performers themselves. The music hall was a universal form of entertainment—even outside English-speaking countries. Unfortunately in this book lack of space has precluded any attempt to place British music hall in its context of international manifestations of the same genre—manifestations which often preceded, matched and frequently far outshone their British counterparts.

Numerous commentators—principally those invoking the ubiquitous 'Good Old Days' aspects—tend to treat Victorian music hall as if it provided entirely musical entertainment, with the 'Variety Virus' entering the scene only in the 1890s, whereas in fact the word 'Variety' had been used in its modern theatrical sense long before the phrase 'music hall' was coined to describe the entertainment rather than the building in which it took place.

There was, however, a definite and significant difference between post-1843 and pre-1843 music hall—the cult of personality. What in fact happened was that although there were stars in all branches of popular entertainment before 1843, their names were not as frequently recorded as their successors', whose rise to fame coincided with, and was usually caused by the development of modern advertising techniques and the spread of popular national and local newspapers. These factors coupled with the growing compilation of archives—both public and private and containing all types of ephemeral material—meant that, even though the coverage of music hall was far sparser than the coverage of legitimate theatre, it was documented to a certain extent, although (like its modern manifestations) not as fully as would be desirable.

Unfortunately much of the documentation available was provided by agents, and the performers themselves who were less concerned with the exact facts than they were with creating an attractive image of their product. Their evidence, and that provided by non-music-hall autobiographers mainly concerned with demonstrating in an early chapter what jolly types they were in their youth—a peculiarly British phenomenon—is useful, but it is frequently repetitive and contradictory or lacking a sound historical perspective. Usually they assume also that the reader has seen what is being described and so do not go into full details of the buildings or the performance. Often, therefore, the best accounts of music hall are to be found not in the writings of those specifically dealing with it, but in books and newspaper reports dealing with general and social matters of the day. The selection following, therefore, is derived from a much wider range of sources than has hitherto been provided when the development of music hall in Britain has been assessed.

Music hall did not, of course, finish in 1923. All that happened then was that the names of the performers were changed, and the methods of presentation, the styles of music and costume altered to suit prevailing taste, fashion and convention. These changes had happened frequently before, and have occurred frequently since. In 1923, however, the changes were more drastic as the phenomenal success of the pre-1912 stars and style of performance had caused a petrifaction of the genre into a static 'old fashioned' form, unacceptable to the post-war generation looking for something completely new and more in tune with modern times.

Obviously it would not be possible to cover every aspect of the subject under review, and so the most significant events and the more important personalities have been chosen, with the stress on those aspects of music-hall history dealt with either only in passing, or not at all in previous histories, for example, the architecture and interior decoration of the halls; provincial halls—in particular the social setting; finance and the laws under which halls operated. But above all the emphasis has been on the sense of continuity in the period up to 1923, and this as Samuel MacKechnie observed of his *Popular Entertainment Through the Ages* (the best balanced account of music hall available) 'has been paramount among the factors which prompted the omission or inclusion of details'.

Fortis Green   DAVID F. CHESHIRE
London

CHAPTER ONE

THE RISE OF MUSIC HALL

The origins of music hall and drama are identical. A person wishes to entertain a crowd by means of story or action; he forms an arena either natural or artificial; a crowd gathers and the entertainment commences. Initially the amateur, or professional, entertainers either worked for themselves or for the community—usually in religious ceremonies. Their non-religious audiences were drawn from the ordinary people, but royalty, the aristocracy and the upper classes were attracted by the performers, and either made use of itinerant entertainers, or engaged sole use of those that attracted them particularly. Fools established themselves as a special group and they (and the court jesters) were granted privileges and given purposes too complicated to discuss here. This pattern of development and the types of performers concerned are common to all races and all ages. This non-dramatic form of entertainment in particular was associated with eating and drinking. Erasmus: PRAISE OF FOLLY, *written 1509, translated by Betty Radice (1971)*

However, there are some men, especially old men, who are more given to wine than to women, and find their greatest pleasure in drinking parties. Now whether a party can have much success without a woman present I must ask others to decide, but one thing is certain, no party is any fun unless seasoned with folly. In fact, if there's no one there to raise a laugh with his folly, genuine or assumed, they have to bring on a 'jester', one who's paid for the job . . . What was the point of loading the stomach with . . . fancy dishes and titbits if the eyes and ears and the whole mind can't be fed as well on laughter, jokes and wit ? . . . And all the usual rituals of banquets, drawing lots for a king, throwing dice, drinking healths . . . singing . . . dancing, miming . . .

As soon as public ale-houses and taverns were established in Britain, music was provided as well. Geoffrey Chaucer included a description of a solo tavern entertainer in THE CANTERBURY TALES, *written c1387, in a version by Neville Coghill (1951)*

There was a parish clerk
Serving the church whose name was Absalon.
His hair was all in golden curls and shone;
Just like a fan it strutted outwards . . .
He used to dance in twenty different styles . . .
He played a two-stringed fiddle, did it proud,
And sang an high falsetto rather loud
And he was just as good on the guitar.
There was no public-house in town or bar
He didn't visit with his merry face . . .

1 *Saxon gleemen from Joseph Strutt's 'The Sports and Pastimes of the People of England,' 1801*

Pleasure Gardens

Following the Restoration of both the monarchy and large-scale public entertainments in 1666, a new amusement-venue was established—the pleasure garden. In 1732 the old Spring Gardens were re-opened under their more famous title—Vauxhall Gardens. Peter Kalm: KALM'S ACCOUNT OF HIS VISIT TO ENGLAND ON HIS WAY TO AMERICA IN 1748, *first published in Stockholm in 1753, translated by Joseph Lucas (1892)*

9th June, 1748. Vaux-Hall. In the evening I went with some of my acquaintance to Vaux-Hall, to see the much-vaunted pleasure garden, where the youth of London, almost every evening in the summer, divert themselves . . . At 6 o'clock in the evening, they begin to assemble, when the music commences at 7 or 8 . . . with a very large number of different kinds of instruments, among which is also an organ . . . When they have played for some time, there appear Chanteurs or Chanteuses . . . When they have continued for a time, there is an interval . . . when those who have come out there either promenade in the garden or sit down at one of the many tables there are, and have brought to them various foods and drinks, wines, confitures, punch, meat, apples, fruits &c, which are all tolerably dear . . . No man or lady enters the garden without paying a shilling at the entrance. After that anyone is free to buy anything or not. One can in the meantime listen to the music, walk about, see and be seen, without any further cost. As soon as it begins to be a little dusk, lamps are lighted up . . . There are here ready all the statues and ornaments which are used in gardens . . . the means of . . . earning money are manifold. Here the musicians and men and women singers earn their subsistence. Here those make large profits who sell various kinds of provisions. Rowers and hire-coachmen are well satisfied with this institution, because they have a large profit out of the large number of people going and coming thither and thence . . . The owner, who leases out this pleasure-garden to those who make all these arrangements, is said to gather a pretty penny . . .

After 1800 entertainers from the gardens also appeared at the song-and-supper rooms. After 1800, the gardens' popularity declined, and they were closed in 1859. Vauxhall and Ranelagh (its close rival) were for fashionable society, but there were pleasure gardens available to the less well-off, both in London and the provinces, or for those disinclined to venture south of the Thames. These pleasure gardens were usually attached to either a public house or a spa. And by the 1830s variety in all but name was being staged at Bagnigge Wells. There was also a garden at Sadler's Wells, but there it had always been a subsidiary to the main attraction—a musick house.

Music Houses

In Elizabethan England the music room, or music house, was the area in a large house, tavern or theatre, set aside for the musicians to perform in, usually out of sight of the audience. But in Jacobean England they had already become separate establishments. In a play 'The Fatal Dowry' (c1632) by Philip Massinger and Nathaniel Field, there is a character described as 'a Singer and Keeper of a Musick House' who is referred to not as mere innkeeper but as a 'gentleman . . . well received amongst our greatest gallants'. Ironically the spread of music houses was helped by Oliver Cromwell. Organs removed from churches under his puritanical regime were bought by tavern keepers and installed in specially built rooms. After the Restoration, music houses proliferated. T. Cromwell: HISTORY AND DESCRIPTION OF CLERKENWELL (*1828*)

None of these, and there were many, particularly in the suburbs of the metropolis, appear to have attained and preserved the celebrity of SADLER'S MUSIC-HOUSE, which was a wooden building, erected on the north side of the New River Head some time before 1683 . . .

The typically music-hall decorations and audience were already apparent at Sadler's Wells. Ned Ward: WALK TO ISLINGTON WITH A DESCRIPTION OF NEW

2 *Variety in all but name at Bagnigge Wells Tavern*

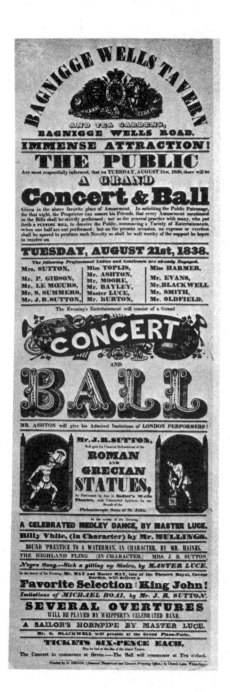

TUNBRIDGE WELLS AND SADLER'S MUSICK-HOUSE (*1699*)

We enter'd the House, were conducted up Stairs,
Where lovers o'er Cheesecakes were seated by Pairs.
The Organs and Fiddles were Scraping and Humming,
The Guests for more Ale on the Tables were Drumming . . .
We began to look down, and examine the Pit,
Where Butchers and Bailiffs, and such sort of Fellows,
Were mix'd with a Vermin train'd up to the Gallows.
As Buttocks and Files, House-breakers and Paddlers,
With Prize-Fighters, Sweetners, and such sort of Traders;
Informers, Thief-Takers, Deer-Stealers, and Bullies,
Old Straw-hatted Whores with their Twelve-penny Cullies,
Some Dancing and Skiping, some Ranting and Tearing,
Some Drinking and Smoaking, Some Lying and Swearing;
And some with the Tapsters, were got in a Fray,
Who without paying Reck'ning were stealing away.
Which made Lady Squab, with her Moonifi'd Face,
By the side of the Organ, resume her old place;
With hands on her Belly, she open'd her Throat,
And silenc'd the Noise, with her Musical Note . . .
Then up starts a Fiddler in Scarlet, so fierce . . .
To shew what a Fool he could made of a Fiddle . . .
Then in comes a Damsel drest up in her Tinsy . . .
Arm'd Amazon like, with abundance of Rapiers,
Which she puts to her Throat, as she Dances and Capers.
And further, the Mob's Admiration to kindle,
She turns on her Heel, like a Wheel on a Spindle;
And under her Petty-coats gathers such Wind,
That Fans her, and cools her, before and behind.
The next that appear'd, was a Young Babe . . .
In Dancing a Jig, lies the chief of his Graces,
And making strange Musick-house Monkey-like Faces.
Then in a Clown's Dress comes my honest Friend Thomas,
Who looks by his Bulk to be Lord of the Domus;
He cocks up his Hat, draws his Heels to his Arse,
And makes his own Person as good as a Farce . . .

In 1765 Thomas Rosomon pulled down the old building and built a brick theatre. T. Cromwell: HISTORY AND DESCRIPTION OF CLERKENWELL

In fitting up the interior, every attention was paid to accommodating the audience with liquor during the performance; and for that purpose the seats had backs, with ledged shelves at the top, so as to secure the bottles for each row of visitors . . . The terms upon the which this objectionable trait . . . was for many years continued, are thus expressed in a bill of 1773: 'Ticket for the boxes 3s which will entitle the bearer to a pint of Port, Mountain, Lisbon, or Punch. Ticket for the Pit 1s 6d. Ticket for the Gallery 1s either of which, with an additional sixpence, will entitle the bearer to a pint of either of the aforesaid liquors.'

Already the type of seating and refreshment arrangements of the late Victorian music halls had been established.

Fairs
Thomas Frost: THE OLD SHOWMEN AND THE LONDON FAIRS (*1874*)
About this time [1684] there was introduced at the London fairs, an entertainment resembling that now given in the music-halls, in which vocal and instrumental music was alternated with rope-dancing and tumbling. The shows in which these performances were given were called music-booths, though the musical element was far from predominating . . .

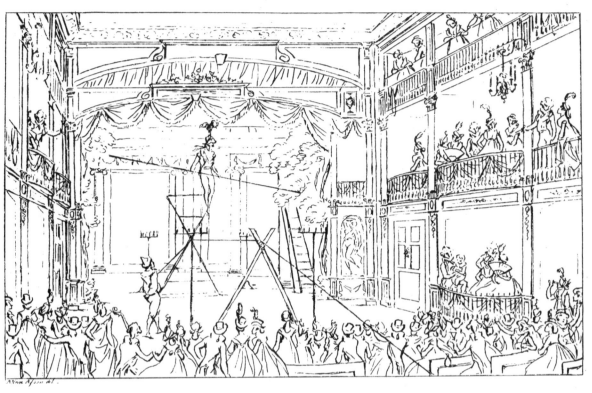

3 *'Rope dancing at Sadlers Wells' 1794. An etching by Antonio Van Assen. The 1765 theatre with a perambulating audience and with seats with ledges at the lower right*

But fairs in general, and music booths in particular, were already under strong fire because of their alleged demoralising influence. In 1700 the lord mayor and aldermen of the City of London resolved that no booths at all would be allowed at Bartholomew Fair—the most famous fair in England held annually at Smith-field, London. A group of lessees petitioned the lord mayor, and he licensed most of them, but the proclamation specifically ordained that none were to be permitted for use as music booths. Thereafter the fairs all over England began to run down. The Industrial Revolution made their use as a labour exchange (or slave market)

less necessary; moralists managed to suppress the entertainments; the public wanted something newer and more regular—it found it in music hall.

Singing Rooms

Informal clubs for music-making (usually madrigals) were established during the Elizabethan period. Often these were centred on barbers' shops where instruments and music were provided to divert customers waiting their turn in the chair. These gatherings were gradually put on a more organised basis. Sir John Hawkins: HISTORY OF MUSIC, VOL V

In . . . 1762, a society for the improvement of vocal harmony was established by a great number of the nobility and gentlemen, met for that purpose at the Thatched House Tavern in . . . Westminster, by the name of the Catch Club. As an incentive to the students of music they gave prize medals to such as were adjudged to excel in the compositions of canons and catches . . . [Motto on medal: Let's drink and Let's sing together]

Over seventy years earlier Ned Ward had described less-elevated catch-singers whose efforts were even closer to those of the frequenters of the song-and-supper rooms, usually regarded as the most immediate ancestors of music halls. THE LONDON SPY COMPLEAT (*1704*)

Accordingly we stept in and in the kitchen found half a Dozen of my Friend's Associates . . . down we sat, and when a Glass or Two round had given Motion to our Drowsy spirits, and we had abandoned all those careful Thoughts which make Man's Life uneasie, Wit begot Wit, and Wine a Thirsty Appetite . . . Songs and Catches Crowned the Night, and each Man in his Turn Elevated his Voice to fill our Harmony with the more Variety.

Initially these glee-clubs consisted of members and select guests entertaining themselves. But outstanding performers soon manifested themselves, and gradually groups of 'stars' evolved. It was not long before singing rooms attracted the opprobrium previously attached to the singing booths at the fairs, but the attacks had a new slant, for to some moralists the rooms were among the most prominent factors preventing the British working-class from gaining education and thus permanent release from the drudgery of factory-work which drink and song only temporarily relieved. Indeed some politically inclined commentators intimated that there may have been a nefarious purpose behind the singing rooms. J. W. Hudson: THE HISTORY OF ADULT EDUCATION (*1851*)

The allurements held out to the working-classes at

many of the beerhouses by means of organs and other musical entertainments, were found to be great rival attractions [to the foundation of Salford Literary and Mechanic's Institution in 1838].

William Cook Taylor took a more favourable view of the rooms. TOUR IN THE MANUFACTURING DISTRICTS OF LANCASHIRE (*2nd ed 1842*)

The operatives of Manchester have shown their taste and capability for higher enjoyments than smoking and drinking. I have gone into some of the concert-rooms attached to favoured public-houses which they frequent, and I have never been in a more orderly and better-behaved company. The music was well selected, the songs perfectly unobjectionable; the conversation, in the intervals between the pieces, not only decorous, but to some degree refined, and the quantity of liquor consumed by each individual very trifling. But I have also been in houses where music was prohibited, and the scenes which I witnessed will not bear description.

Most of the singing rooms were modest affairs. But owners began to build more elaborate edifices during the 1830s, and give them fancy names. Benjamin Disraeli: SYBIL OR THE TWO NATIONS (*1845*)

A sharp waiter, with a keen eye on the entering guests, immediately saluted Gerard and his friend, with profuse offers of hospitality insisting that they wanted much refreshment; that they were both hungry and thirsty; that if not hungry, they should order something to drink that would give them an appetite; if not inclined to quaff, something to eat that would make them athirst. In the midst of these embarrassing attentions, he was pushed aside by his master with, 'There go; hands wanted at the upper end; two American gentlemen from Lowell singing out for Sherry cobler; don't know what it is; give

them our bar-mixture; if they complain, say it's the Mowbray slap-bang, and no mistake. Must have a name . . . name's everything; made the fortune of the Temple [of the Muses]; if I had called it the Saloon, it would never have filled and perhaps the magistrates never have granted a licence.

'Music Hall'

The adoption of an apparently ultra-respectable name for a form of popular entertainment was undoubtedly behind the use of 'music hall' to describe the rooms in which popular entertainment was presented after 1850. Previously 'music hall' had been used to describe what would now be considered concert halls eg The Music Hall, Store Street, London which specialised in recitals of sacred music, and the music halls in provincial towns

4 *The interior of Holder's Concert Hall on the opening night—24 June 1846—showing the pre-concert dinner. The room was enlarged in 1857 but continued to present glees, madrigals and opera until 1876 when variety acts were introduced. Its name was changed to the Gaiety in 1886*

which served a variety of purposes when the magistrates would issue a licence, eg The Music Hall, Three Crowns Corn Market, Warrington, where on 4 September 1788 (according to a bill in the British Museum) a musical romance and a farce were presented. Mander & Mitchenson maintain that 'The Grapes, Southwark Bridge Road, was the first tavern concert room to call itself a Music Hall'. But the names used to describe the actual halls (ie concert room, harmonic hall, music hall) were varied according to the whims of the owner, as was the type of fare provided. Thus 'The Builder', 22 December 1855, described the new Evans room as a 'Music-hall'; Charles Morton presented a concert version of Gounod's 'Faust' at the Canterbury, and as late as 1863 James Hole used 'music hall' to distinguish 'a Concert Hall of the highest class of music' from 'low beerhouse rooms' in 'The Working Class of Leeds'. The members of Disraeli's 'Two Nations' were the singing rooms' and music halls' main patrons. For the upper classes and the lower classes shared a love of sport, convivial entertainment, ingenious indecencies and drinking, all of which were eschewed by the more strait-laced middle classes. Most singing rooms were usually either for the upper class or lower class patrons, but there were certain rooms—particularly in London—where all classes mingled. Blanchard Jerrold: LONDON (1872, repr 1972)

I suppose that in the old times [ie the 1840s] . . . men had a decided taste for the underground. To feel most at ease . . . they must work their way under the earth's surface. For in those days, cellars and shades and caves were the chosen resorts of roystering spirits of all degrees . . . whither knowing young gentlemen of fortune from Oxford and Cambridge, would occasionally repair to show their friends how very acute and penetrating they were.

5 The exterior of Henry Holder's Rodney Inn and Concert-Hall, Birmingham, 1846

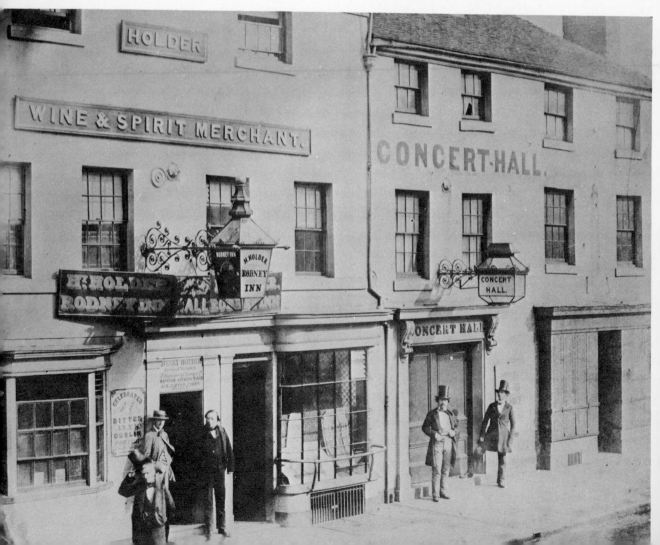

Among the most notorious of these rendezvous was 'The Mogul' in Drury Lane, London—later the site of the Middlesex Music Hall. The Hon F.L.G.: THE SWELL'S NIGHT GUIDE THROUGH THE METROPOLIS *(c1840). This little book, aimed at country cousins who aspired to be swells, also directed attention to places where 'civility and attention' were not available, and to places where the entertainment was traditional but not 'typically' Victorian.*

Who has not heard of the 'Mogul'. The Colossus of the minor singing rooms! the glory of the Teppsichorians of Drury Lane! and the greatest link of the cockney between music and the drama? There are few places in the Metropolis that have acquired such a degree of notoriety, as the 'Great Mogul' . . . Mr. Cook the present proprietor, having taken the house somewhere about . . . 1825, finding the concert room much too small to accommodate the numbers who flocked there, he, in 1836, at the expense of £4,000 constructed his present room, and rebuilt the house, now capable of holding between three and four hundred persons. Concerts are nightly performed here, and there is no room in the metropolis better conducted of the same size, few so well. The house has gained some name for the excellent quality of its grog, and for civility and attention it must yield the palm to none . . .

THE THREE TUNS. Not to know this despicable resort of prostitutes and thieves, would argue an ignorance of London which the swell is most anxious to avoid. The landlord . . . demands, and takes in person, threepence for admission to his concert room; which is nightly filled by the flash women who infest Fleet Street and its environs. The songs sung are of the most beastly description; the men picked from the cab stand . . . The ladies who sing, or attempt to do, have evidently other ways of picking up their bread, more profitable but less irksome . . .

['Paphian Revels'] These places of voluptuousness are situated in the neighbourhood of Waterloo Place, and Waterloo Road, and are almost entirely frequented by such of the frail sisterhood as are of French nationality . . . about 'The witching hour of night' commence what may really be termed the orgies of the Cyprian Goddess. Girls of every state, from complete nudity to the half dressed, go through the most voluptuous exhibitions—and perform the most spirit-stirring dances!

Edmund Yates described the most publicised singing room in HIS RECOLLECTIONS AND EXPERIENCES *Vol I (1884)*

'Evan's late Joy's'—the pun was intentional—had a reputation for higher-class singing than its rivals, but the principal attraction to its all-male audiences was the opportunity to add their own obscene interpretations to popular songs of the day. Gradually, however, a change took place in the style of entertainment. Ribald songs were banished, and instead the choruses were sung by choirs of young boys whose sweet fresh voices were heard with charming effect in the old glees and madrigals. The little room was too small for the audience; it was pulled down [in 1855] and a vast concert-room built on its site with a stage where the singers stood, and an annexe—a comfortable . . . hall, hung with theatrical portraits . . . where conversation could be carried on, and it was by no means necessary to listen to the music.

The public thronged to the concert-room—there was a private supper-room in the gallery, looking down on the hall through a grille where ladies could hear the songs and could see without being seen—and the annexe became, and continued for several years, a popular resort for men-about-town. The landlord —John 'Paddy' Green—ought to have made a fortune; but he did not, and the introduction of music-halls, where women formed the larger portion of the audience, was the signal for his downfall.

6 'One o'clock A.M.: Evan's Supper Rooms.' Wood
engraving from a drawing by William M'Connell
reproduced in G. A. Sala's 'Twice Around the Clock',
1859. The platform-like stage with footlights and the
performer's number on the programme; the chairman
and his cronies at a table facing the all male audience,
and the grills through which the ladies watched, are
clearly visible

The fame of Evans carried over into the music-hall
era, and on its site Harold Scott inaugurated the modern
revival of Victorian Music Hall in 1937.

CHAPTER TWO

THE ESTABLISHMENT OF MUSIC HALL: 1843-1890

Theatres and the Music Hall

Initially most popular performers did not present their acts in formal theatres. Occasionally, however, they did appear within plays and Shakespeare was only the most prominent author to complain of clowns extemporising lines, while both he, and all his contemporaries and predecessors were glad occasionally to leave a space for the clown to enter and present his 'act', or to make use of speciality acts if the occasion arose. Indeed, when Lord Leicester's Men performed in Denmark in 1586 they were referred to as singers and dancers rather than actors. There was no clear demarcation apparent as far as professionals were concerned. Stephen Gosson described some typical acts within a play in PLAYS CONFUTED *(1590), and is the first recorded user of the word 'variety' in this context*

For the eye, beside the beauty of the houses and the Stages, he sendeth in gearish apparel, masks, vaulting, tumbling, dancing of jigs . . . juggling . . . nothing forgot, that might serve to . . . ravish the beholders with variety of pleasure.

From the Restoration period onwards, however, plays were more tightly constructed and rarely left room for extraneous matter. 'Variety' acts, were, therefore, presented as curtain-raisers, during intervals or as afterpieces. Gradually special entertainments, pantomimes, were developed to cater for British audiences' love of variety. Indeed the greatest name in pre-1843 'variety'—Joseph Grimaldi—was a pantomime clown. Vaudeville theatres presented similar entertainment, eg a bill in the British Museum for the City Vaudeville, London, 11 April 1831 shows that they presented two burlettas, a vaudeville, a performance on the musical glasses, a dramatic recitation and sketch in one act 'in which Mrs Glindon will sustain seven different characters'. Much of this variety was presented (particularly in London) in an effort to circumvent the ban on the presentation of 'legitimate' drama anywhere except at

This distinction was accepted, but caused endless difficulty during the following decades. Thus music formed the main part of the entertainment presented at the quite splendid halls erected all over the country. The most famous of these was Canterbury Hall in Lambeth opened by Charles Morton in 1851. Oratorios and selections from operas were among the major attractions at the Canterbury and elsewhere, and were the nearest the halls could get to dramatic performances. Licensing discrepancies soon became obvious. In 1852 a select committee was appointed by the House of Commons

to examine into the system under which public houses, hotels, beershops, saloons, coffee houses, theatres, temperance hotels, and places of public entertainments are sanctioned and regulated, with a view of reporting whether any alteration of the law can be made for the better preservation of public morals, the protection of the revenue, and for the proper accommodation of the public.

The committee heard a wide range of witnesses—all of whom still used the phrases 'concert rooms' and 'singing houses' rather than 'music hall'. The rooms' demoralising effect was discussed at length, but they also had their defenders. R. A. Stephen, Superintendant of Police, Birmingham: REPORT (1854)

Chairman: Can you say . . . that there is a growing taste for this sort of representation?—There is a growing taste.

And it is not connected with gross indulgence?—No: far from it.

It is rather as a substitute?—I should say so.

The dog-fighting and bull-baiting . . . have diminished?—Diminished a great deal; bull-baiting I have never known a case of, dog-fighting I have.

It used to prevail very much in Birmingham?—Yes.

In 1853 two acts were passed which boosted the halls'

7 Charles Morton (1819-1904) as the 'Grand Old Man of the English Music Hall' in the 1890s

the two Patent Theatres—Drury Lane and Covent Garden, a monopoly established by Charles II, reinforced by the Theatre Act 1737, and broken by the Theatre Act 1843. This act also accelerated the rise of music hall in the generally accepted modern meaning of the term. For the saloons were informed by the Lord Chamberlain that to secure his licence in future they would have to be run as theatres and be described as such. At the same time he presented their owners with alternatives—either they could stage plays but not serve refreshments in the auditorium, or they could serve refreshments in the auditorium but not stage plays.

8a *The exterior of the 1862 Collin's Music Hall, Islington, London, showing frontage of rooms at left of plan*

8b *Sketch plan of Collin's Music Hall, Islington, believed to have been prepared by The Metropolitan Board of Works following an initial survey in 1882 under the provisions of the Metropolis Management . . . (Amendment) Act, 1878 which enforced stricter fire precaution. The proposed alterations were not carried out, and the hall was rebuilt on a larger scale in 1885. The plan shows what is essentially the original building except for the saloon adjacent to the auditorium—only one wall is visible at the top right-hand corner. NB The line of the balcony is not indicated*

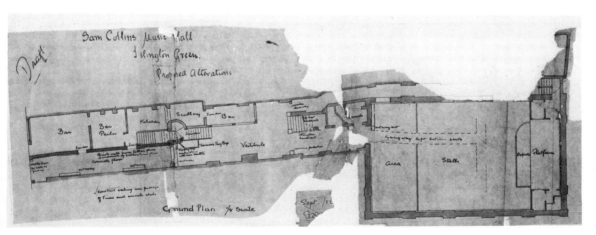

*audiences even more. One suppressed betting houses; the
subsequent presence of bookmakers shouting the odds
during the performance at the Canterbury where many
of their customers congregated emphasised the close
connection between the turf, the ring and the theatre in
Regency and Victorian England. Illegal bookmakers
centred their London activities on York Corner, Waterloo
Road. The other abolished the tax on press advertisements. Halls and supper rooms could draw the attention
of the less raffish to their existence discreetly and cheaply.
In fact increasing attention was given to the nocturnal
entertainment centres in the press in general. A significantly worded account of the rebuilt supper-room at
Evan's appeared in* THE ART JOURNAL, *April 1856*

Artistic improvements in our places of public resort
are of so uncommon a kind that we feel bound to
devote a few words to a supper-room reconstructed
at the back of Evan's Hotel, Covent Garden, and
which may be considered one of the most elegant
rooms in London . . . A very few years ago it
would have been impossible to have alluded to this
improvement at all; but to the present proprietor, Mr.
Green, is due the honour of having elevated the moral
tone of its amusements and made them unobjectionable.

*The revelation in the 1851 census that half the popu-
lation of Britain now lived in towns, and the fact that
many more children were being educated either formally
in schools, or informally by the increasing number of
journeys being made for pleasure by all classes, following
the immense commercial success of the special excursion-
trains from all parts of the country to the Great Exhibi-
tion of 1851, meant that there were more potential
writers and performers seeking employment. The trains
also meant that performers could 'tour' much more
speedily and conveniently. The halls also benefitted as
music was now an integral part of elementary education.*
MINUTES OF THE COMMITTEE OF THE COUNCIL ON
EDUCATION REPORTS BY HER MAJESTY'S INSPECTOR OF
SCHOOLS 1852-3, Vol II, GENERAL REPORT, . . . FOR
1852 *(1853) by T. W. M. Marshall*

It is known to your Lordships, and Mr. Mayhew's
painfully interesting work on London Labour and
London Poor has made it known to all readers of
that book, that it is an habitual practice in public
houses of an inferior stamp, all over the country, to
have frequent musical entertainments of a low and
immoral character, for which performers are in great
demand. A certain cultivation of the voice and a due
knowledge of exciting and profligate songs, in the
best of which 'sentiment' is allied with indelicacy,
and humour is depraved into 'slang', constitute the
requisite qualifications; and it is worth reflecting
whether that semi-professional skill which the
ordinary method of teaching music in schools is
calculated to impart and which appears to be often
all that is aimed at, may not possibly become a fatal
gift to those that acquire it.

*Two areas provided most of the singers to the early
halls: the East End of London, where in addition to the
native British, immigrants from the continent, and many
travelling showmen following the dissolution of the
Bartholomew Fair, had settled, forming a lively group
of people—the Cockneys; and Lancashire. However all
areas provided entertainers for local, and, sometimes,
national, consumption, while in the heyday English-
speaking acts came not only from all parts of the United
Kingdom but also from the colonies (particularly
Australia) and the United States of America.*

New Buildings
*The introduction of horse omnibuses in 1855 enabled
people to move out of their immediate neighbourhoods in
search of work and entertainment, and it was becoming
safer to venture out at night (on main thoroughfares)
following the introduction of more efficient street-lighting*

24

and police-forces. *So not only were <u>new venues estab-</u> <u>lished, but existing buildings were improved.</u>* BUILDING NEWS *15 April 1859*

Such is the growing taste for musical entertainments, that the feeling for it is extending in the far east of the metropolis as well as at its western portions. The Canterbury Hall, Weston's and the Raglan, have now become noted places of resort for the votaries of Apollo; and now it appears that Mr. Wilton, of Wellclose-square, near the London-docks, having found his old music-room totally inadequate to accommodate the great influx of visitors who nightly were in the habit of congregating at his well-conducted concerts, has been compelled to erect a hall on a more extended scale. Calling in, therefore, the assistance for Mr. Jacob Maggs . . ., Mr. Wilton has just had finished one of the best music-halls in London.

Internally, the building is 75 feet in length by a width of 40 feet, and 39 feet in height from the floor to the crown of its arched roof. In planning the room, the architect, no doubt having especially acoustic purposes in view, has maintained in a high degree, curved lines; thus the ceiling is segmental, and the stage is backed by a semicircle, crowned with a semi-sphere, while the other end of the room forms an alcove, the result of this being that the hearing throughout the whole area is perfect. The whole of the decorations of the interior have been well executed in carton pierre and papier mache, by Messrs. White and Parlby, 49 and 50 Great Marylebone-street, and the magnificent sun-burner of cut-glass, suspended

9 *Anonymous sketch of the interior of an unidentified music hall, c1890, clearly showing the disposition of the bars, the fence between stalls and pit and the double 'fauteuils' in the stalls*

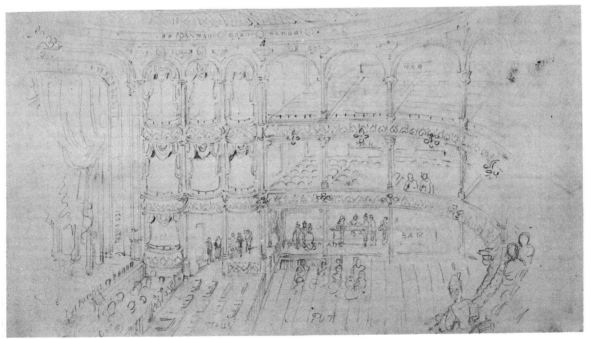

from the centre of the ceiling, together with four other cut-glass chandeliers are from the well-known manufactory of Messrs. Defries and Sons, of Houndsditch. The large central sun-burner consists of 300 lights, besides the new sunlight of 100 jets, which, we understand, is the largest ever made, being composed of no fewer than 27,000 pieces of cut-glass.

A central shaft has been provided over this large sun-burner, so that however crowded the apartment may be, not the slightest inconvenience is felt by oppressive heat, as is too generally the case in concert-rooms, where large numbers of persons are congregated.

The ceiling of the hall is divided into 25 panels, and the walls are formed into five double recesses on each side. These recesses have semicircular arched heads, over which is an appropriate entablature. The semi-dome over the stage is formed in seven radiating panels, and in its wall are inserted large looking-glasses, in which are reflected the whole extent of the room in perspective. A gallery, 9 feet in projection, runs along the two sides and south end of the room. This gallery is supported by ten enriched columns, and its front is decorated with sculptures, foliage, and scroll-work, in the Italian style, relieved by color and gilding.

Throughout, the enrichments in relief are subdued white, relieved by the gold, grounds being blue and red. These colored and gilded portions have been executed by Mr. Honman in a very satisfactory manner.

Mr. Thomas Ennor, builder, Commercial-road-east, had the contract for the various constructive works. The brass-work of the building, much of which is of a highly ornamental character, together with the gas-fittings, and an illuminated device at the entrance, have all been executed by Mr. Shirley.

Another sign of the times (and a neat Morton publicity stunt) was reported by THE BUILDER *6 November 1858*

It is curious to note the endeavours which are being made to add extraneous attractions to taverns. Thus, in one of those places near King's-cross for instance, the curious traveller who may peep in, will find an Italian-looking saloon—blazing with gas-light—filled with sad objects of humanity and large collections of specimens of natural history. There are the skulls and tusks of phants, stuffed sharks, and other strange fish; the place, in fact, looking more like a museum than a hostelry. In other parts it may be noticed that 'mine host' is endeavouring in other ways to attract custom by some kind of intellectual pleasure.

In Holborn, Covent-garden, and elsewhere, rooms of great size and costliness have been erected, and music and singing are made to lend their attractions. All these arrangements, however, are thrown into the shade by the proprietor of Canterbury Hall, in the Westminster-road, who has built, in addition to a very large apartment for musical entertainments, a handsome picture-gallery, at an expenditure of £5,000 and filled it with pictures which have cost him £10,000 . . . The pictures . . . include 'Noah's Sacrifice', by Maclise; 'Death Purifying the Soul', by Horace Vernet; 'A Danish Family Reading the Bible', by Madame Baumann; 'Mountain Scenery', by Cailcott; 'Marcus Curtius leaping into the Gulf', by Haydon; 'The Advent of Spring', by F. Danby . . . The proprietor says, in a preface to the catalogue,—Although almost every other class of the community is represented at the Canterbury Hall, his chief supporters are to be found among the working classes. If, then, while providing for them the innocent and enlivening enjoyment of music in the hall, the fine-arts gallery can be made the medium for raising in their minds ennobling and refining thoughts, and of creating and fostering a taste for the beautiful, the proprietor feels that his establishment can prefer a fresh claim to public support. This is a new language from such a source, and not without its import. The attraction of the tavern, 'pure and simple', must be fading, since it is necessary to add others of an intellectual character.

As the writer would have realised if he had read Disraeli's SYBIL, *it was (as with so much else) the written publicity that was new, not the 'intellectual character'. At the Temple of the Muses the ceiling was richly decorated and the walls painted in the 1830s.*

The popularity of the halls burgeoned, and, in some areas, to accommodate all those who wanted to get in, twice-nightly shows were introduced in the 1860s— obviously derived from the practice in the Penny Gaffs and Fair-theatres. Sir Richard Mayne, Chief Commissioner of the Metropolitan Police in the REPORT OF THE SELECT COMMITTEE ON THEATRICAL LICENCES AND REGULATIONS (1866) *proved erroneous the usual claim that twice-nightly performances were initiated by Henry de Frece and George Belmont in 1885. He reported having seen places at the east end, where they had two performances in the evening at six o'clock, and at eight; one audience following another.*

In the 1860s halls proliferated in the provinces also. All had similar antecedents to the London ones. Charles Weldon: REMINISCENCES OF MUSIC HALL AND VARIETY ENTERTAINMENTS, MANCHESTER 1864-6 *(2nd ed 1907)*

The London Grand Music Hall was originally established on the site now occupied by the Queen's Theatre. In the early thirties it was known as Hayward's Hotel. In a large room at the rear was held the earliest meetings of the Manchester Glee Club. Previous to its conversion into a Music Hall it was occupied by Dr. Mark and his 'Little Men', and was known as Dr. Mark's College of Music. The Hotel premises comprised a large yard in the rear of the building, with stabling, coach-houses, and the usual appurtenances of an old-fashioned posting house. A light roof of timber was thrown over the yard, some old cottage property and stabling was demolished and a large stage and proscenium erected and furnished with scenery and gas fittings. The yard was boarded over and seated, and the back rooms of the hotel with windows overlooking the yard were converted into private boxes.

The Oxford

In London music hall moved into the 'West End' in 1861. The London Pavilion was opened on 23 February and the Oxford on 23 March. The latter had a chequered career which epitomised that of music hall in general over the next thirty years. BUILDING NEWS, *22 March 1861*

It was a Continental assertion that the English were not a musical nation. To foreigners there was a doubt as to whether we were competent to appreciate music either vocal or instrumental. It appeared to them impossible that such an exquisite recreation should in any way be agreeable to a commercial people, whose sole purpose of existence apparently consisted in making money. Taste may be dormant till called forth by some cause not hitherto known. The present certainly warrants the assertion, for there was a time when good music could only be heard by paying good prices, far beyond the means of the artisan or middle-class tradesman. The Opera, Hanover-square, and Willis's Rooms, were the only places where the compositions of our best masters could be heard. The telling portions of these performances were retailed to the multitude by indifferent street organs; at times by three—at the most four—outside, midnight public-house performances, a cornet taking the leading part, embellishing his performance by the execution of some noisy and impossible cadence, waking the whole neighbourhood with his inharmonious noise. However, out of this evil came good; these street performances, accompanied by wandering minstrels, were taken into the houses, and from that moment dates the birth of the music-halls which are now being erected in every district of London.

10 *Programme showing the main entrance of the 1893 building. A more representative cover than plate 45*

The most important of this class is the one now in course of erection (and rapidly advancing towards completion) at the corner of Oxford-street and Tottenham-court-road, at the rear of the Boar and Castle Tavern—the name of which is to be 'The Oxford'—the old tavern used to be a noted coaching-house, and had very extensive stabling at the back. All the old building has been removed to obtain a site for the music-hall, while the entrance through the tavern has been considerably altered to give more loftiness to the entrance . . ., the crown of which will be about 16 feet from the floor . . . The hall itself is 44 feet wide, 90 feet long, and 40 feet high . . . The promenade and picture-gallery is nicely arranged . . . The building may be fairly considered as the finest one of its class; it is to be regretted there was not better judgment displayed in the decorative part, for should so large a building look cold, it must always appear uncomfortable, and we think the success of the music-halls may be traced to the warm, comfortable appearance they present . . .

The Oxford soon made its presence felt. THE NATIONAL REVIEW (*1861*)

The decay of the street ballad singer . . . we attribute more to the establishment of such places of entertainment as Canterbury Hall and the Oxford, and the sale of penny song-books, than to the advance of education or the interference of the police . . . we do not pretend that they will be any great loss.

BUILDING NEWS, *14 February 1868*

The Oxford Music Hall . . . was destroyed by fire on . . . [11 February] The fire was discovered by the watchman, at about 3 a.m., who found the seats in the right-hand corner of the gallery facing the stage in a blaze. The flames soon spread to the roof and the body of the hall, and in less than an hour the whole of the roof fell in. The destruction fortunately is not so great as in recent fires at similar buildings, and it is stated that there is not a single hole in the flooring caused either by the fire or the fall of the roof. In the cellars beneath the building, an immense quantity of wines and spirits are stored, and had the flames reached these the result can hardly be imagined. The gallery, on which so much material fell, has sustained no essential injury. This is owing to its peculiar construction . . . The gallery is constructed on a principle of leverage, the resisting power being the whole weight of the wall, or super-structure over the end pinned into the wall, while a heavy beam acted as fulcrum—so that only a comparatively small portion was overhanging, and it is all but impossible to have been broken down by the falling materials. We understand the plans and particulars are still in the hands of the architects, Messrs. Finch, Hill, and Paraire, and that there need be no delay in restoring the premises . . .

The hall was not so lucky on the next occasion a fire broke out there on 1 November 1872. THE ERA, *3 November 1872*

The fire we understand was first discovered at 3.55 a.m. by a cabman . . . The situation of the Hall, hidden as it is from the street, favours the probability that some time must have elapsed between the first outbreak and the discovery, so that when the engines arrived the flames had secured a hold which it seemed almost impossible to overcome . . . The stage, the balcony, the private boxes, the massive pillars which formed such prominent features in the architectural beauties of the Oxford, all presented a scene of desolation and disfigurement. Above, nothing stood between us and the sky but the blackened rafters . . .

In the saloons . . . the statues and valuable pictures have suffered but little . . .

The new owner (Morris Syers) reconstructed, and the Oxford was re-opened on 17 March 1873. THE ERA, *23 March 1873*

The first glimpse of the interior reveals that some important changes have been made . . . a splendid promenade in place of boxes, at the back of the balcony . . . makes a most agreeable lounge for those who prefer freedom of action and wish to gossip with their friends between the pauses in the entertainment, and from this spot the best view of the stage and the performance can be obtained . . . A new stage of much larger proportions than the old . . . The footlights are sunk to the level of the stage, and the orchestra placed somewhat beneath it . . . In point of colour and decoration the Oxford may vie with any building in the kingdom. The prevailing tint is light blue [at the Oxford!], the relievo ornaments white, with stencilled decorations upon the walls, and choice salmon tints filling up the spaces. Mr. Homann, the accomplished decorator of the Mausoleum of the late Prince Consort, has executed this portion with exquisite skill . . .

The Oxford thrived for the next two decades, until Syer's death in 1890. THE BUILDER, *4 October 1890*

An order has been made in Mr. Justice Sterling's Court, Chancery Division, for the sale, under provisions of the late Mr. Morris Robert Syers's will, of the Oxford Music-hall. The property consists of one lot, comprising the music-hall, with the adjoining Nos. 18 and 20 Oxford-street, and the fully licensed premises known as the 'Boar and Castle' . . .

In 1892 H. Newson-Smith added it to the syndicate he was in the process of forming—his other halls included

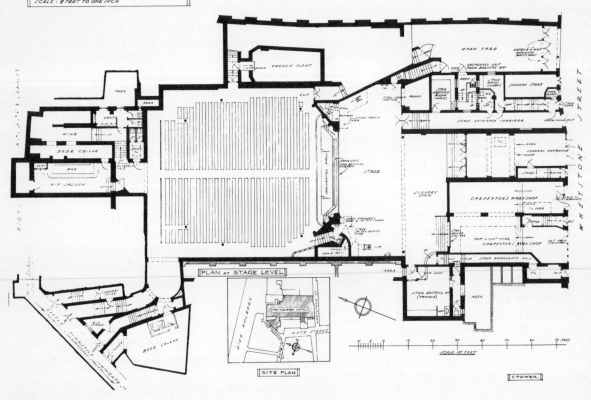

THE EMPIRE MUSIC-HALL
HIGH HOLBORN, W.C.1
AS EXISTING IN 1920.
SCALE : 8 FEET TO ONE INCH.

PLAN AT STAGE LEVEL

SITE PLAN

SCALE OF FEET

C.POWER.

11 *The Empire, Holborn, London as it existed in 1920. Originally built as Weston's Music Hall to a Finch & Paraire design in 1857, altered and redecorated by Lander & Bedells in 1892, new frontage added in 1897 to combine the hall and adjoining public house, and completely rebuilt in 1906. Again Frank Matcham produced a neat design (this time to circumvent rights of ancient lights which prevented the new building from rising above the height of the old) with entrance at circle level and the stalls at the former basement level. The elimination of the pit, the presence of a Soda Fountain, two 'star' dressing-rooms, and a large carpenter's workshop with generous scenery dock adjacent, all indicate the changing pattern of music-hall entertainment for which the owner (Walter Gibbons)*

planned to cater. Damaged by bombing 11-12 May 1941. Demolished 1961

the Tivoli and the Pavilion. *The first building was closed on 4 June 1892, and immediately demolished. Henry Pownell (Chairman of the Middlesex Magistrates) revealed that the Oxford's licence-application was not un-opposed.* SELECT COMMITTEE REPORT (*1866*)

Chairman. Do you find when a new music-hall is going to be opened, that there is an opposition by those who have got licences already?—Yes, constantly . . . When the Oxford Music Hall Company applied for a licence there was very great opposition; all the music-halls, including the Raglan, in Theobald's-road, joined . . . and great expense was incurred in opposing the licence.

On what grounds do they habitually put their opposition?—That there is not sufficient business for another house.

They openly consider it as a question of monopoly?—Yes.

In his replies the Hon S. C. B. Ponsonby revealed that whereas the Lord Chamberlain's department invariably inspected theatres, and plans for theatres—to see if they were structurally and practically as safe as possible—the local justices did not exercise such care over the halls under their jurisdiction. This safety aspect was to become increasingly important as halls became more popular and bigger. Whereas the Lord Chamberlain insisted that theatres should have several exits, halls did (or rather could) not. A Select Committee was appointed in 1876 to inquire into the Metropolitan Fire Brigade, and into the most efficient means of providing for security from loss of life and property by fire in the metropolis. Its REPORT *(1876) explained*

12 *Ruins of the Surrey Music Hall in the Zoological Gardens, Southwark. Designed by Horace Jones for an audience of 10,000 and opened 15 July 1856, it was destroyed by fire in June 1861. Rebuilt and used by St Thomas' Hospital until 1872 when it reverted to theatrical use*

that if the proprietor of a music hall desires to sell spirits or other liquors, he has further to obtain a licensee from the Brewster Sessions of the Division, a matter that has a bearing on this inquiry, because whilst numerous means of egress are serviceable in case of fire, the licensing justices under the Intoxicating Liquor Acts object, in the interest of order, to allow a multiplication of entrances and exits in what are practically public-houses on a large scale.

THE SATURDAY REVIEW, *6 August 1887*

whatever may be said of the London theatres, they are fireproof as compared with the majority of the music-halls . . . In comparing the music-halls with the theatres, it must be remembered that, if the former are much smaller and do not contain as many people as the latter, they unquestionably make up for the difference in size by a more than proportionate amount of danger. In the first place, drinking, which admittedly tends to excite the audience, goes on during the entire performance, and smoking is of common occurrence. Indeed, it is the rule, and not the exception, with the male portion of the audience. Smoking leads to throwing about lighted cigar ends and cigarette ends. And one muslin dress set on fire by a match or a cigar or cigarette end carelessly thrown would create just as great a panic as would take place in a theatre wrapped in flames. The old Oxford Music-hall was, if we recollect rightly, burnt down through carelessness of this kind, and what has happened once may happen again.

The entrance to the Oxford is in Oxford Street. In case of fire, the entire audience might have to leave, as they leave every night, by the one door by which they come in. There is another small exit, as the label says, 'in case of need', on the O.P. side of the stalls; but on the night of our visit it was locked. Another label directs the audience to another door on the Prompt side, which leads on to a small back-yard in

Donaldson's Buildings and through a small, narrow court, blocked with shop-shutters, on to Tottenham Court Road. This door was also locked. Playful little jokes like these may possibly be amusing, but in our judgment should be sternly repressed. Twenty-one stairs lead on either side of the house to the balcony. At the very back of the hall, and quite close to the steps of the balcony, is, according to the label, another extra door. On examination, however, it turns out that the door in question leads down nineteen steps to the small yard in Donaldson's Buildings to which we have referred. In fine, there is but one real exit to the Oxford and that exit is in no way sufficient.

Bad as is the Oxford, it cannot compare in any way with the Trocadero. This house is situated in Windmill Street, and its one entrance is divided into four doors. It is hardly possible to believe not only that all these four doors open inwards, but also that, even in this hot weather, three out of the four doors were firmly barred and bolted up . . .

Increased Popularity

In 1878 London's theatres consisted of: Drury Lane and Covent Garden holding 4,000 each; 45 theatres licensed by the Lord Chamberlain, holding an aggregate of about 80,000; 10 theatres licensed by the divisional magistrates as they were outside the Lord Chamberlain's jurisdiction holding about 38,000 between them. Music halls existed in even larger numbers holding even more people eg the Middlesex magistrates licensed 347 halls holding altogether 136,700, divided into the following categories: 3 First-class with accommodation ranging from 15,000 to 20,000; 6 Second-class, 2-3,000; 13 Third-class, 800-1500; 53 Fourth-class, 300-700; and 272 smaller places consisting of public-house concert rooms, harmonic meeting places etc. In addition the Surrey magistrates licensed 61 music halls holding 32,800 south of the Thames, and even the City of London licensed 6 halls holding 6,400.

In 1879 an event took place which was to have a

significant effect on two types of entertainment: two major music-hall stars, Herbert Campbell and G. H. MacDermott were included in the cast of the pantomime at the Covent Garden Theatre. The following Christmas their success was repeated by Arthur Roberts and James Fawn at Drury Lane. These annual appearances in pantomimes by an increasing number of major music-hall stars also introduced them to middle-class audiences (particularly wives and mothers) hitherto unacquainted with them except by hearsay. When these audiences began to go to the halls they demanded something other than the steady procession of striking, but indifferently staged soloists. They wanted spectacular variety with scenery, ballet and special effects. The erection of the old-style hall petered out, and henceforward more theatre-like buildings were built, although (in London at least, and quickly elsewhere) municipally imposed regulations were the main cause of the sudden decline, and change of form, principally because The Metropolitan Management and Building Acts Amendment Act of 1878 called for the closer inspection of music halls from the safety angle. Many of the smaller and older ones (including Evans) lost their licences. Owners of others eventually took the opportunity to redevelop their properties. The country, however, was in the midst of the Great Depression when real prices fell by about 40 per cent. But whereas in the more notorious 1931

13 The Empire Music Hall, Newcastle. Architects, Messrs Oliver & Leeson. Opened 1890. Another view of this hall was included in Richard Southern's 'Victorian Theatre' (1970) where it was, however, incorrectly described as having existed in this form since 1837

débâcle the working classes were the principal sufferers, the first Great Depression worked to their advantage. Though prices fell, wages remained steady, and so the real income of an average family increased by about 60 per cent. Nevertheless there was considerable political unrest in the eighties, and although attendances at, and profits of, the existing halls rose remarkably, the owners preferred to keep the existing buildings in use, making slight adjustments were necessary to comply with new regulations. Not until the depression began to pass in 1896 did another wave of building—on an even grander scale—commence. The occasional new hall was built during the Depression, eg The Empire Music Hall, Newcastle-upon-Tyne, 1 December 1890. A music hall had been opened in Newgate Street in 1878 as part of the Royal Scotch Arms Hotel; the new Empire was based on a conversion of it. A letter to Mander and Mitchenson from T. Middlebrook when they were attempting to identify an uncaptioned photograph of the Empire is an exemplary delineation of what distinguished a music hall from a theatre at that time

A close examination indicates the following:—

(1) It is a music-hall (with 'Palace of Variety' leanings); the stage floor has no traps and there are number boards which look rather as if they had been designed to fit an existing proscenium and not an integral part of new work.

(2) The building has been recently redecorated and, possibly, partly rebuilt. (New wallpaper, paintwork and upholstery). There are signs that it is not a completely new building; for example, there are cracks (one puttied up) in the panels of the draught screens behind the pit seating.

(3) It has electric lighting, with gas secondary which was still not common in 1891. It may be noted that the unusual pattern floats are mounted in a wider trough, extending well to either side of the fittings, and not metal lined as it would probably have been for gas. This suggests that the trough was originally built for a gas installation and that the boarded lining shown (lining through with that of the stage floor) was laid as part of a general overhaul of the premises. Both seem quite unmarked by use.

(4) There appears to be a glazed partition on the O.P. side which probably separates a stalls bar from the auditorium. There are no signs of fittings or shelves to hold glasses on any of the seating, suggesting that drinking in the auditorium was not permitted.

(5) The pit and stalls are separated by a continuous barrier extending to the auditorium wall on the P. side, at least.

(6) The plasterwork to the ceiling, proscenium and rester joints is obviously of first-class workmanship and represents considerable capital expenditure. The auditorium walls on the other hand are without any architectural embellishments; particularly noticeable where the tiers abut against the proscenium wall.

Particularly unusual features include the following:—

(1) The contrast between the conventional shape of the circle and the almost 'square' gallery shape.

(2) The curve of the section of the gallery facing the stage; this is followed through in the line of the ceiling above.

(3) The subdivision of this section of the gallery into private boxes.

(4) The unusual depth of the side of the proscenium arch.

(5) The two parallel metal rods or tubes fitted immediately below the ceiling over the centre of the auditorium. They appear to be an afterthought and are probably not important.

I'm fairly confident that it was not in London . . . Some odd things went on when the Council was very new but the following points appear to contravene the London regulations in force at that time:—

(1) There seems to be no exit from the stalls on the P. side.

34

The Empire, Leedo.   E.B.

(2) Instead of the 3'-6" required by the Council the gangways between seats are only about two feet wide. The gangway in the stalls seating has obviously been arranged by removing one seat from each row, leaving fixing lags and screws projecting into the gangway.

(3) Loose chairs are shown in the P. side stalls gangway.

(4) There are no EXIT signs visible over any of the doors.

(5) The premises are equipped with glass bottle

14 The Empire, Leeds. Architect, Frank Matcham. Opened 29 August 1898. On view behind a rather more fantastic proscenium arch than usual is a stock drop-scene used at random throughout the show—little attempt being made to match the scene with the act

'fire grenades' instead of hydrants or fire buckets. These things were not particularly efficient and neither our records nor those of the London Fire Brigade give any indication that they were ever accepted for places of public entertainment in London . . .

CHAPTER THREE

THE HEYDAY OF MUSIC
HALL: 1890-1912

The type of show, and the performers, of this period have established themselves as 'real old-time music hall', even though music no longer predominated, and the entertainment was frequently (and more accurately) called variety, indeed the first 'history of the music halls from the earliest period to the present time' (1895) was called 'The Variety Stage'. Some of the west-end public, however, thought that the 'real' music-hall atmosphere had been dissipated, and in private clubs (eg The Prince of Wales' at the corner of Coventry Street, London) 'song-and-supper room' shows were revived in the 1890s. Moralists continued to protest about the immorality of the halls, and P. Anderson Graham claimed that they were among the factors that had caused one of the newer 'social problems of the day'. THE RURAL EXODUS *(1892)*

When the railway company issues its posters announcing a cheap excursion for one, two, or three days to town, Hodge immediately becomes alert.

This is the pleasure in which he can get value for his money. It would be interesting to know the average cost of one of these expeditions . . . a young gamekeeper tells me that not many would leave home with less than three or four pounds in their pockets . . .

But the importance of the cheap trip lies in its educational more than in its economical aspect. From it the rustic learns much that the schoolmaster could not teach him . . .

Long ago the men would have talked of country themes. The news they would have discussed would have been the bastardy and poaching cases at the Petty Sessions . . . the outlook for turnips and hay, the qualities of horses . . . It is not that sort of conversation which goes on today. The absorbing topics are reminiscences of the latest trip to town. Hodge has been to the cheap theatres and music-halls, and is a keen critic of actresses and music-hall 'artistes', whose merits and demerits he discusses most keenly . . . The cheap trip has revealed to

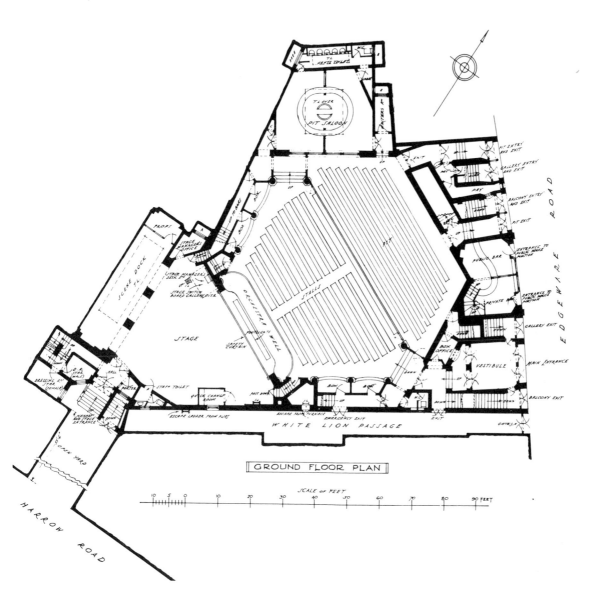

15 *The Metropolitan, Edgware Road, London as it existed in 1903. Architect, Frank Matcham. Cunning use of an awkward corner site. No direct access to the bars and saloon or from the pit to the stalls*

him a contrast between living and a state of torpor, and he prefers the former. The cheap trip has opened his eyes.

The Empire, Leicester Square

In 1892 another Select Committee was appointed to investigate the current state of the theatrical licensing acts. The committee was mainly concerned with activities on the stage, but much was made of the fact that the improved 'moral tone' of the performances had had a 'beneficial' effect on the morals of the audience. In certain areas traditional mores prevailed, for example the promenade at the Empire, Leicester Square.

Prostitution and the theatre had always been closely linked. But at music halls the link was even more obvious, while at Wilton's it was blatant: the gallery could be entered only through the brothel inside which the hall was built. Leicester Square had become the centre of the trade by the nineties and the Empire, firmly established as 'a club' for colonial officials, soldiers, civil servants, 'advanced' clergymen as well as for the aristocracy, young bloods, Bohemians, and ordinary music-hall goers, found that its promenade was a major attraction. It was, therefore, properly organised. No attempt was made to ban 'respectable' prostitutes from entering, but strong efforts were made to ensure that nothing unseemly happened—in the theatre. Unfortunately for the management two less-than-worldly Americans were solicited, and stormed out to inform an English acquaintance of the outrage. Their acquaintance was the formidable campaigner against vice, Mrs Ormiston Chant, who took the opportunity to oppose the renewal of the Empire's licence at the October meeting of the Licensing Committee of the London County Council. DAILY TELEGRAPH, *11 October 1894*

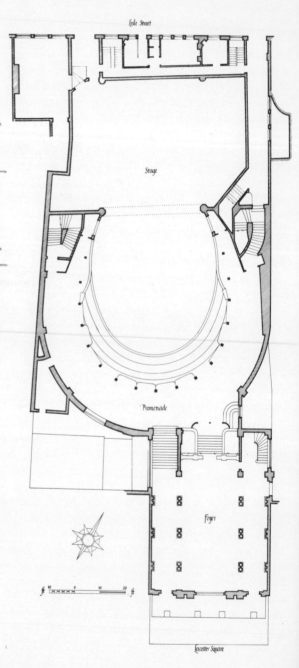

16 *Empire Theatre, Leicester Square, London. Architects, J. & A. E. Bull. Opened 17 April 1884. This 1891 plan of the dress circle level clearly shows the size of the notorious promenade*

Mrs. Chant stated that her attention was first called to the Empire early in the present year by two American gentlemen . . . They were so shocked that she determined to visit the theatre, but did not do so until July, when the Living Pictures had made so much stir. Early in the evening there were comparatively few people in the promenade, but after nine o'clock the number increased. She noticed young women enter alone, more or less painted, and gorgeously dressed. They accosted young gentlemen who were strangers to them, and paid little attention to the performance. She herself was so quietly attired that one of the attendants exclaimed to a woman, 'You had better mind how you behave tonight—there are strangers about'. (Laughter) . . . Mrs. Annie Hicks gave evidence on behalf of the opposition . . .

Do you object to women going to places of entertainment alone?—No; I think that women ought to be able to go into any assembly alone.

Exactly on the same footing as men?—Quite so.

And not be interfered with so long as they conduct themselves with propriety?—Yes . . .

Mr. Collins, described as a tea merchant in London and Liverpool, deposed that he had gone to the Empire nearly twenty times during the last three months, and on one occasion counted well-nigh 180 women of objectionable character. The Empire was, he thought, notoriously a show place for that kind of thing . . .

Mr. Gill, opening the case for the applicant, commented upon the testimony which had been produced in opposition to the license. Though well-meaning people, perhaps, the witnesses were persons of the most violent and extreme views, who, instead of attending to their own affairs, presumed to look after the morals of others and dictate what sort of entertainment should be offered to the London public. A number of gentlemen of large capital and great enterprise had been lavish in their expenditure in order to put on the Empire stage the best performance

that money could possibly produce, with the result that the theatre was constantly full, so that any reflection upon the entertainment was equally a reflection upon the spectators. Immoral characters were perfectly entitled to go to the promenade, and so long as they conducted themselves with propriety they ought not to be interfered with. There had not been the slightest complaint of their behaviour since the renewal of the license by the County Council. The authorities at the Empire took every possible precaution in the interests of the proper management of the theatre, and he urged the committee not to be led away by the extremely improbable stories that had been told them.

Mr. George Edwardes, managing director of the Empire, examined by Mr. Gill, said . . . In front of the house we have a large staff responsible for the good conduct of the people entering the theatre. It is nearly 100 strong, and headed by a retired inspector of police and several sergeants. Practically everybody is inspected before being allowed to enter, and nobody goes in without paying for admission. A sergeant and detective are in the promenade seeing that the women there behave themselves properly. If anything like marked accosting is observed, first the woman is cautioned, and for a second offence she is taken out of the house. The same thing applies to men. Women are frequently prevented from entering . . .

Much similar evidence was heard before the committee decided to recommend the renewal of the licences, on the conditions that the promenades be abolished and the seats occupied there disposed of to the satisfaction of the Council, and that no intoxicating liquors was to be sold in the auditorium. It may be noted that the capital involved was presented as evidence for the Empire. Mrs Ormiston Chant: WHY WE ATTACKED THE EMPIRE (*1895*)

The Secretary of the London Trades' Council placed

himself and his supporters on the side of the money-lender, the greedy capitalist, and monopolist, the heartless, fashionable ruffian who employs the pimp and procuress . . . and all the conscienceless crew who were using the tragic picture of the starving ballet-girl and scene-shifter to screen the portly figures of the grabbers of 75 per cent . . .

Q.Cs. acting for the Palace asking for a licence for the use of the Palace Theatre as a music-hall said [on 12 October 1892] that the Empire opposed their request because 'it would interfere with our 70 per cent profit'. The Q.C. for the Empire admitted 'that great damage will result to the Empire Theatre Limited, from the granting of such a licence.'

The full LCC meeting to consider cases in which renewals of licences had been opposed altogether, or granted subject to certain conditions, was not held until 26 October, and during the interim the argument raged furiously in the press, pulpits, meetings, and newspapers. The 'Daily Telegraph' gave it massive coverage, and the catchphrase 'Prudes on the Prowl' was a headline to the letters on 13 October responding to their anti-Chant leader of 12 October.

Many of the letters to the press were repetitive, pseudonymous and concerned (like most of the protest meetings) with the amount of unemployment the Empire's closure would cause. DAILY TELEGRAPH, *15 October 1894*

A largely attended meeting . . . was held last night [by] the Theatrical and Music-hall Operatives Union . . . to discuss the situation . . . Mr. Charles Thorogood . . . moved, 'That this meeting deplores the decision of the Licensing Committee of the London County Council to impose upon the management of the Empire Theatre conditions which render it impossible to keep the theatre open, and thus throw a large number of people out of employment' . . . the resolution . . . was carried unani-

mously. A member of the Empire staff said that at that place the stage employees alone had 322 children depending upon them, beside their wives. There were 140 union men employed on the stage.—Mr. George Shipton, secretary of the London Trades Council, said . . . He would do his best to bring their case before London workmen generally. Although it was the Empire today, they did not know what house it would be tomorrow . . .

Last night a general meeting of the members of the north-west branch of the London Cabdrivers' Trade Union was held . . . The president . . . thought that every assistance should be given to Mr. Edwardes to prevent those persons who were taking such a great interest in the morals of Londoners ruining, not only public places of amusement, but the cab industry . . .

Mr. George Edwardes . . . said the decision of the Licensing Committee to altogether close the promenades and prohibit the sale of intoxicating liquors in the auditorium, should it be enforced, meant absolute ruin to the establishment and would compel them to close its doors. On the previous night, he had given a formal fortnight's notice to employees who numbered some 670, and upon whose labours fully 3,000 mouths depended for their daily bread . . .

'Advanced' churchmen engaged in the debate. The Church and Stage Guild, lead by the Rev Stewart Headlam and the Rev Stanley Gresham expressed deep regret at the action of the Licensing Committee. Mrs Chant's original objections became so obscured that she had to restate her case. DAILY TELEGRAPH, *18 October 1894*

All that I want . . . is to clear certain of the music-halls of the unclean features which debar decent folks from attending and enjoying the performances. A short time ago I was at the Palace Theatre of Varieties in London, and I was charmed and delighted with what I saw. As to the living pictures, they were beautiful, and there were only three to which I objected. It is significant that these were received almost in silence by the audience. All the rest were enthusiastically cheered.

Do I object to ballet? Nothing is further from my mind. I don't object to tights, as such. I know that when you dance very vigorously you must not be impeded by clinging petticoats about your ankles, or even about the knees. If need be, I think I could devise a costume which would give this freeness and yet clothe the limbs, although I am not one of those who think it a shame to have legs. It is the motive at the back of it all, and the obvious suggestiveness, which makes the thing evil. We have no right to sanction on the stage that which if it were done in the street would compel a policeman to lock the offender up . . . The whole question would be solved if men, and not women, were at stake. Men would refuse to exhibit their bodies nightly in this way.

On the 26th Mr Murphy QC opened for the Empire, reiterated scornfully the opposition's evidence, repeated the unemployment argument, and cast doubt on the good faith of Mrs Chant. She replied, DAILY TELE-GRAPH, *27 October 1894*

To me the action of the manager of the Empire has been astonishing. The very night after the decision of the Licensing Committee was given he called his employees together, and told them that they would be thrown out of employment because the committee insisted upon the structure of the promenade being altered. In doing that Mr. George Edwardes gave the whole of his case away, for he virtually stated that if the promenade were done away with and the sale of drink stopped in the auditorium ruin would fall upon the Empire, and admitted that the takings at the door barely covered the expenses of the theatre. We are, therefore, forced to the conclusion that if you take away the market for vice and the sale of drink, the directors will no longer be able to pay the shareholders their enormous dividends . . .

Mr John Burns Labour MP

It is, I consider, our duty to tell the theatrical and music-hall profession that it would have been better if the directors of the Empire had come to the table, and, withdrawing all inspiration from the bogus agitation outside, thrown themselves upon the sense of justice and fair treatment of the Council . . . We are told we are ruining property; but in the City the other day a 10s share went for 70s. The whole thing is nothing more or less than a commercial rig to coerce the Council into a breach of their duty to the citizens. We have been told also that the Empire employees will be thrown out of work, and we have been asked what will become of them? Mr. Edwardes knows perfectly well that if Mr. Henry Irving can mount a scene on the stage in less than twenty minutes—if he can prepare one of his 'living pictures' in less than a quarter of an hour . . . [Edwardes] has only to put a hundred carpenters into the Empire at a quarter-past twelve at night and in a few hours they can re-arrange the promenade so as to comply with the demands made by the architect at the request of the committee . . .

The council decided to support their committee's decision to order the abolition of the promenade by 44 votes to 22, and to ban the sale of drink in the auditorium by 43 to 21. The theatre re-opened on 26 October. At the end of an attempt at a normal programme, Edwardes spoke. THE STAR, *27 October 1894*

'I have merely to announce to you that owing to the decision of the County Council'—(Here for some time nothing could be heard but passionate anathemas of the Council and cries of 'The dirty dogs!' 'Out with them!' and 'Foul bigots!' mingled with renewed cheering 'for the Empire'.) 'I have merely to announce . . . that in consequence of that decision the Empire will close after tonight. ('Shame!') Believe me—I say this in sorrow rather than in anger—we have not had opportunity or time to reply to all the unfounded charges made at the Council meeting; but we have one consolation, and that is a great one—that we have your sympathy, and that of the London people.'

The speech closed, enthusiasm and passion alike found vent—the former in cheers for Mr. Edwardes and the directors, given over and over again, and the latter in hoarse, incoherent yells of execration against the County Council. Strong men went pale and ghastly with rage, while dilettante youths tried to emulate their demonstrativeness, and succeeded to the extent of a shrill cry of 'Dem'd shame'.

The promenade was 'altered', and the Empire reopened on 3 November with another massive demonstration, in which Winston Churchill played a leading part—as he vividly recalled in 'My Early Life' (1930). PALL MALL GAZETTE, *5 November 1894*

All . . . [acts] had the applause of an audience which had apparently come only to cheer itself hoarse; but the time was utilised by many for the inspection of the promenades . . . The bar at the back had been shut off from the promenade by means of a screen of woodwork covered with canvas . . . gradually the crowd began to attack the screen. Well dressed men—some of them almost middle-aged—kicked at it from within, bursting the canvas, but hardly affecting the woodwork. The attendants—most of whom might have played the giant in a country show—watched in helpless and amused inactivity. Finally there was an attack on the canvas,

which was torn away in strips, and passed throughout the crowd, every one endeavouring to secure a scrap of it as souvenir. Mr. Hitchens, the manager, attempted argumentative remonstrance, but was carried away by half a dozen enthusiasts. Then the woodwork of the screen was demolished by vigorous kicks from both sides. The crowd had already cheered itself hoarse, and now began to go out into London, brandishing fragments of the screen . . .

Cinematograph

The Empire was the scene for the next, and in many ways, the most momentous event in the brief history of British music hall. On 28 December 1895 the Lumières presented the first public film show in Paris, and almost immediately in London, where the leading British pioneer soon joined them. H. G. Hibbert: FIFTY YEARS OF A LONDONER'S LIFE *(1916)*

Trewey, the juggler, and exponent of comic expression with the aid of a flexible felt hat, brought the Lumière apparatus to London . . . music hall agents and music hall managers were incredulous. Trewey resorted to the home of the scientific toy—the Polytechnic [Regent Street, 20 February 1896] and was looked upon as having achieved the finality of his mission. But he persisted. He arranged an afternoon session at the Empire . . . [on 9 March] He soon insinuated the cinematograph to the evening programme there.

By the end of 1897 cinematograph shows had been given in nearly every music hall, but, although worried by the gramophone, managers and financiers seemed unperturbed by films, which were seen as a passing novelty, and no real threat, especially as nearly all films were still 'documentaries' and silent.

Trade Unionism

In 1897 The Metropolitan was rebuilt. In 1900 Moss

opened the London Hippodrome as a circus, and a firm of stockbrokers (Keith, MacAllister) established themselves as 'specialists in theatre, music hall and [NB] cinema shares and securities', undoubtedly inspired by the recent registration of Moss' Empires Ltd. with a capital of £1,000,000. Around 1900, however, halls in less well-favoured areas began to founder, eg in 1904 the Empire, Ardwick Green, Manchester, became the first large music hall to be converted into a cinema. But in London the Holborn Empire was re-built in 1906. In the same year the Conservatives suffered a massive

17 *The non-pictorial side of the programme at the Tivoli London, 13 November 1905, shows that the dominance of advertisements in such publications is long established*

election defeat. Labour won twenty-nine seats, and with another twenty-four associates amongst the Liberal majority, ensured that a wave of 'social' legislation was undertaken. Within a fortnight of the election, the Variety Artists Federation (a Trade Union) was formed, and within a year music hall underwent its first strike. DAILY TELEGRAPH gave the event massive coverage. On

18 *Polemical pre-strike cartoon. 'The Performer', 27 December 1906*

23 January 1907 it summed up the situation, and how it had developed

War has been declared between those who control and those who provide the entertainment given in the music-halls of the country. No time has been lost in bringing matters to a crisis in London. On Monday evening there was no performance in five of the six variety houses under the direction of Mr. Walter Gibbons. At one of these, the Holborn Empire, a performance was given, but there was no 'second house'. The artists, orchestra, the stage hands, and most of the other employees, had decided to strike because of an alleged breach by the management of an agreement which was arrived at between the parties. Yesterday there were rapid and serious developments, of which the most notable was the determination to induce the artists engaged at all the halls belonging to the syndicate of which Mr. G. Adney Payne is the head to join in the movement and to refuse to perform. The effect of this decision was that the area of dispute was immediately widened . . .

Until the end of last week there existed three separate organisations formed to safeguard the interests of those employed at music-halls—the Variety Artists' Federation, the National Association of Theatrical Employees, and the Amalgamated Musicians' Union. These, while retaining their independent machinery, have now combined under the title of the National Alliance of Music-hall Artists, and this combination was solidified on Sunday evening at the meeting held in the Surrey Theatre under the presidency of Mr. W. Crooks, M.P. Before this combination was effected the

Variety Artists' Association had entered into negotiations with Mr. Walter Gibbons, and maintain that he agreed to the payments of half a day's wage for matinees—all the halls controlled by Mr. Gibbons are run on the two houses a night system—to artists engaged at all the halls belonging to him and to incorporate in contracts certain other demands put forward on behalf of the employees. Apparently no agreement was arrived at with regard to unexpired contracts, and Mr. Gibbons, holding that the arrangement should only apply to contracts after July 14, declines to sign contracts of which the terms have been fixed by the association. Accordingly the artists and others engaged at the six halls mentioned were 'picketed' by representatives of the federation, and many of them refused to take their turns . . .

Now as to the demands of the employees . . . As summarised in the 'Performer', the official organ of the Variety Artists' Federation, the terms which they ask all music-hall proprietors to agree to are as follows:

1. That at all their halls, or halls under their contract, working two shows a night, all matinees shall be paid for at the rate of one-twelfth salary for each matinee.

2. That no artist shall be transferred from one hall to another without his, her, or their consent.

3. That 'times' shall not be varied after Monday in each week without the artist's consent.

4. That all disputes shall be referred to a board of arbitration, such board to consist of two nominees of the proprietors and two nominees of the V.A.F. executive committee, and an independent chairman to be nominated by the above four nominees.

5. No commission to be stopped where artists are booked direct.

6. No bias or prejudice to be shown to any artist who has taken part in this movement . . .

DAILY TELEGRAPH *published some performers' views*

on 24 and 25 January

MARIE LLOYD who is taking a very active part in the struggle, stated emphatically that the Alliance meant to fight tooth and nail, and she had every hope that they would win. 'A wrong impression has got abroad,' she remarked, 'as to the position of the "star" artists. It is said that they are quarrelling with the

19 *Strike hand-bill*

Music Hall War

Twinkle, twinkle, brilliant Star!
Oh, I wonder where you are.
With the V.A.F so bright,
You will **not** show here to=night.

The following Stars will not appear at the Payne and Gibbons' Halls till the dispute is settled:—

MARIE LLOYD	MARIE KENDALL
MARIE DAINTON	VICTORIA MONKS
VESTA VICTORIA	GUS ELEN
ARTHUR ROBERTS	R. A. ROBERTS
JOE ELVIN	ALEC HURLEY
CLARK & HAMILTON	PAUL MARTINETTI
JOE O'GORMAN	FRED GINNETT
JOCK WHITEFORD	WAL PINK
HERBERT SHELLEY	LEONARD MORTIMER

Printed by the Co-operative Printing Society Limited, Tudor Street, London, E.C., and Published by J. B. Williams, 9, Great Newport Street, W.C.

managers on their own behalf. That is not so. We can dictate our own terms. We are fighting not for ourselves but for the poorer members of the profession, earning from 30s to £3 per week . . .' ALEC HURLEY [reducing the issue to a more personal level]. What we are really fighting . . . is a music-hall trust. If the policy which has caused all the trouble succeeds, it will be impossible for artists to earn a living in London at all. At present the average artist is really at the mercy of the manager. He has to sign a contract to appear at a certain hall for six nights, and he is not allowed to perform at any other hall in the neighbourhood for twelve months thereafter. In many cases it practically means ruin. I myself have an engagement at a North-East London hall, and I have been asked to undertake another shortly afterwards in a neighbouring district. I mean to accept it . . . VESTA TILLEY. Personally, she had no grievance, nor had any of the leading artists, but she knew of the grievances of those whose turns were in less demand . . . HARRY RANDALL. This agitation has been going on underground for ten years, and now that it has come to the surface the matter is not likely to be allowed to rest until a substantial change has been secured . . . HARRY FRAGSON was strongly of opinion that the artists are entitled to a re-adjustment of terms, although even now they are not quite so hardly used as their brethren in France used to be . . .

Invited to explain the situation [OSWALD STOLL] . . . declared that very few of the artists knew what they were fighting for, and many were appalled at the result of their secret meetings, held in the true spirit of irresponsible adventure. Verbal fireworks by similar men had caused sad havoc in the United States, and it was a vital article in the constitution of the present American federation that they must not go on strike.

Questioned as to the reason for the strike, Mr Stoll said: 'It is an indisputable fact that every per-former with an iota of real entertaining power is getting, not only a living, but a handsome living, while many whose vocation should be anything but that of public entertainers are able to maintain a standard of living which thousands of trade unionists would envy.'

Have you noticed the statements of Miss Marie Lloyd?—'Oh, yes: Her utterances are so grossly exaggerated that it is to be hoped they are due to an innate partiality for dramatic effect, rather than to that truth which constitutes her value as an artist . . .'

Do the public quite understand the meaning of what is called the 'barring clause' in the agreements of artists?—'The barring clause is really the foundation of the "variety" superstructure. It means that managers pay a large salary for the exclusive services of an artist. Performers who appear anywhere and everywhere soon tire the public, but when they play at one place alone they speedily assert their true value . . .'

DAILY TELEGRAPH, *28 and 30 January 1907, reported that the Alliance had held mass meetings. At the first enthusiasm was unbounded, especially when the announcement was made that a lease had been taken of the Scala Theatre, with a view of running it as a music hall, and turning the adjoining buildings into a music-hall exchange. But at the second it was* resolved to postpone the opening of the Scala Theatre performances until Monday, Feb. 11. The decision is significant in perhaps more ways than one. In the first place, it seems to indicate that the resolution to open the Scala to-morrow had been taken without adequate regard to the facts of the situation. In the second, it may be taken as showing that at the variety artists' headquarters the view is held that the end of the strike is not quite so near as some of the more enthusiastic members of the alliance profess to believe.

By 5 February DAILY TELEGRAPH *had to observe that*

the music-hall strike is practically at an end. For five hours yesterday representative managers and 'star' artists discussed the question of a settlement, and at the conclusion of the meeting it was announced that an agreement had been reached . . .

There is little doubt, however, that the action of the 'stars' must lead to the collapse of the strike movement. As a result of the unbending attitude of the National Alliance officials, a strong third party has been formed . . . [Including] Arthur Roberts, Marie Lloyd, Little Tich, Vesta Tilley, Harry Randall, Wilkie Bard, George Robey . . .

Late last evening the alliance issued the following statement, signed by the chairman, Mr. Mountford, and the joint secretaries, Mr. Johnson, Mr. Williams, and Mr. Gerald:

There is no truth in the rumours of an approaching settlement of the music-hall war. There is no 'third party' in the National Alliance. The result of the conference between certain members of the Variety Artists' Federation and the managers has in no way

affected the strike. The happenings of the next few days will doubtless convince everybody of the fact that the strike is still in progress . . .

DAILY TELEGRAPH, *12 February*

The great entertainment with which the National Alliance of Variety Artists hope to set London agog . . . [took place] at the Scala Theatre last night amid plenteous signs of enthusiasm. If one were to be severely critical, one might say at once that the performance was disappointing. If by 'stars' are meant variety artists of the first rank, then was the title somewhat of a misnomer. It might more appropriately have been designed 'A Night Without the Stars', for the stellar array was by no means of the first magnitude . . . Nevertheless, there were plenty of 'stars' scattered about the house . . . Miss Marie

20 *Arbitrators in the music-hall strike. Left to right: Walter Payne, Henry Tozer, Oswald Stoll, Henril Gros, Arthur Roberts, Edward Browne, W. C. Steadman M.P., Wal Pink, Alderman I. Mitchell LCC. From W. H. Boardman's 'Vaudeville Days'*

Lloyd viewed the performance from a box . . .

On 15 February DAILY TELEGRAPH *had to report that*

last evening the Music Hall War entered upon a new phase, when all the pickets were withdrawn from the twenty-two halls 'barred' as a result of the strike . . . Mr. George R. Askwith was yesterday . . . asked to officiate as arbitrator. It is understood that he has accepted.

He took four months to make his final arbitration. DAILY TELEGRAPH *carried a precis of his report on 15 June*

Mr. [G. R.] Askwith declares that where, under the terms of an engagement, an artist may be transferred from one to another theatre of an associated group with the consent of the artist, such consent shall not unreasonably be withheld.

Existing contracts often provide that managers may in their absolute discretion close their houses, when salaries shall not be payable. The arbitrator decides that such withholding of salaries shall only be justified where the theatre is closed by reason of national mourning, fire, epidemic, strikes, lock-outs, disputes with employees, or order of the licensing or any local authority. No salary shall be payable if the artist is ill or in default . . .

Where the contract says the artist shall appear at all matinees weekly without the payment of any additional remuneration, artists shall in future only be called upon to perform at such matinees as were the usual weekly practice at the time the contract was made; any additional matinees to be paid for . . .

[On the barring clause] which was largely the cause of the music-hall artists' strike, the abritrator gives a number of most important decisions:

(a) The barring of theatres of varieties for a period after the termination of any engagement, except for not more than two weeks after the termination of an engagement in provincial towns, is abolished.

(b) In a London West-end theatre of varieties, if the engagement be for at least fourteen weeks during any period of twelve months, and a salary of at least £40 per week, the contract may include conditions that the artist can be barred from performing at other theatres . . .

His award was the basis for all future contracts and agreements. Improved awards were made in 1913 and 1919.

Even the strike did not deter enthusiastic speculators from building new halls. An account of the establishment of one in the NORTHAMPTON INDEPENDENT, *18 November 1911, includes incidents and financial practices encountered, and employed, in the erection of many provincial halls*

When the news was first given . . . that a music hall was to be built in Abington Street, Northampton, many people were horrified. Dismayed residents in the neighbourhood petitioned the powers that be, a deputation waited on the Town Council, and there was almost as much fuss as though a pestilence instead of a palace was going to be dumped in our midst . . . The approximate cost is about £30,000 . . . Mr. Simmons [managing director] outlined the type of entertainment envisaged 'Mainly variety with a sprinkling of drama. We shall rigidly cater for a family audience and provide a high-class entertainment which parents can bring their children to without any fear that their susceptibilities will be disturbed. We shall tolerate nothing common or objectionable' . . .

We may add that a considerable proportion of the capital has been subscribed but a few shares remain to be taken up, and anyone desirous of having a financial interest in the undertaking should apply to the Secretary . . .

The theatre was due to open in August. When the Northampton Theatre Syndicate was successfully sued by Edwin Barwick, a character artist claiming compensation for a cancelled date, at Lambeth County Court on 21 October, Mr Simmons explained that the opening of the theatre had been unavoidably delayed by the coal, railway and Thames lightermen's strikes. It was opened on 9 December 1912 in the presence of the mayoress and other dignitaries—an indication of the boost to respectability the Royal Command Performance of 1912 had given the music hall.

Royal Command Performance

Queen Victoria had been an ardent opera and circus-

21 *The New Theatre, Northampton. Architect, John Wilkins. An eminently respectable classical frontage for a variety theatre on a quiet provincial, high street near a Carnegie Public Library, facing a convent, and with the parish church opposite its stage-door, and the church school at its rear*

goer, but had never visited a hall. Edward VII had privately and soon after his coronation commanded Dan Leno to appear before him at Sandringham. In 1909 he visted the Empire and the Alhambra openly, but not formally, with Queen Alexandra. His sudden death meant that George V, also a frequent hall-goer in his youth was responsible for giving music hall its accolade, or (as some say) its death blow. A full account

49

appeared in THE TIMES *2 July 1912, under headlines*
which again emphasise that the terms 'music hall' and
'variety' were used interchangeably

THEIR MAJESTIES AND MUSIC HALLS

COMMAND PERFORMANCE

THE ART OF THE VARIETY THEATRE

Last night the art of the variety theatre received a
new and a signal honour—an honour, too, which the
art has thoroughly earned by its steady progress
from obscurity (not unmixed with obscenity) in
'caves' and 'cellars' to general favour as an indis-
pensable form of harmless amusement housed in
sumptuous palaces . . .

The scene in the house to which they lent their
distinction must have convinced them that vulgar
display is by no means a characteristic of the modern
music hall. Three million roses sounds, we admit,
like overdoing it; but the three million roses used
. . . in decorating the house—not to mention the
wisteria, the flower-wreathed coloured lights, the
beautiful marble decked with baskets and other
Renaissance ornament in gold—were disposed with
so much fine taste that the effect was one of light and
airy elegance. The Royal box itself, with its roses,
carnations, and other real flowers, its exquisite
painted panelling and graceful pillars, was a work of
art of which no age or place, however courtly, need
have been anything but proud. And as for the
audience, if, in boxes, stalls, and dress circle, it was
not absolutely representative of the average music-hall
audience at one of the larger houses—if the men wore
tails and white ties instead of jackets and black ties,
and the ladies appeared in something even more
elaborate than the elaborate evening dress which is
familiar in the stalls of a variety theatre—the audience
looked, on the whole, more like an average music-hall
audience than an audience at a gala night at the opera.

And overhead tier upon tier was packed with the
genuine enthusiastic music-hall audience—some of
whom had been waiting since the small hours of the
morning to gain admittance . . .

THE PROGRAMME

The Palace Orchestra, overture, 'Britannia'
Pipifax and Panlo ('Humpsti Bumpsti')
Barclay Gammon, 'Rule Britannia' and 'In the
  Shadows'
The Palace Girls, 'A Fantasy in Black and White'
G. H. Chirgwin
Joe Boganny's Opium Fiends, 'Five Minutes in
  China Town'
Fanny Fields, 'The Happy Little Dutch Girl'
Cinquevalli, 'The Human Billiard Table'
Harry Tate, 'Motoring'
Vesta Tilley, 'Algy, the Piccadilly Johnnie'
La Pia, 'The Dance of Fire' and 'The Spirit of the
  Waves'
Little Tich, 'Popularity' and 'Big Boots'
Arthur Prince and Jim, nautical ventiloquial scena
The Palace Orchestra, selection, 'Melodious
  Memories'
Alfred Lester and Buena Bent, 'The Village Fire
  Brigade'
Clarice Mayne with J. W. Tate, 'I'm Longing for
  Some One to Love Me'
George Robey, 'The Mayor of Mudcumdyke'
Charles T. Aldrich, eccentric humorous juggling
David Devant, sleight of hand
Wilkie Bard, 'The Night Watchman'
Anna Pavlova, assisted by L. Novikoff and members
  of the Imperial Russian Ballet, 'Le Cygne',
  'Papillon', Divertissement, 'Valse Caprice'
Harry Lauder, 'Roamin' in the Gloamin' '
Cecilia Loftus, 'Impressions of Artists'
Variety's Garden Party. Produced by Albert Toft
'God Save the King', solo by Harry Claff

That list includes no one who is not among the
most talented and eminent of the thousands who

provide nightly amusement in the music-halls of the country; and though it would be possible to point to omissions of famous names and of popular branches of the art (no one will regret the absence of performing animals, but there are no trick bicyclists and no wire-walkers), the programme is pretty thoroughly representative . . . Their Majesties followed the whole programme with evident interest and amuse-ment; though, like most of us, they must have found some items far too short and others far too long. Indeed, not a few of the performers seemed to be a little overawed by the august occasion, and to lack the sparkle of the oddity which endears them to the nightly patrons of the music-hall; and the slowness of some meant drastic reduction of the time allotted to others . . .

There was considerable dispute over two notable omissions—Marie Lloyd and Albert Chevalier. Chevalier (and Bransby Williams) were undoubtedly omitted as they had already given individual command perfor-mances, Marie Lloyd possibly because the king was not one of her admirers. But H. G. Hibbert shrewdly observed in FIFTY YEARS OF A LONDONER'S LIFE *that*

We shall never get the inner history of the Command Performance of 1912—a fierce contortion of personal ambition, a bitter antagonism of jealousies, a triumph for nobody in particular . . . In the event, there was a picturesque crowd, a rather dull performance which could not, by the wildest stretch of imagination, be called typical of the English music hall, but above all, there was another brilliantly contrived world-wide and sensational advertisement for the Palace Theatre.

CHAPTER FOUR

THE DECLINE OF MUSIC HALL: 1913-1923

After the 1912 Royal Show music hall's fortunes declined sharply. The respectful reception accorded to the performers at the Palace by a predominantly establishment audience did not please those who admired music hall for its vulgarity and brash common touch. Charles E. Hands: 'A Common Person's Complaint' DAILY MAIL, *25 November 1913*

There is one trifling but obvious fact that seems to have been overlooked in this latest discussion as to the morality of the music-hall.

It is that there are not any music-halls. In the sense that the music-hall is a place of popular entertainment, a place for the amusement and enjoyment of the common people, it has ceased to exist in London, and there are very few vestiges left of it anywhere in the kingdom.

If this fact had not already been recognised the circumstances of this controversy would demonstrate it. The moralists and the artists are fighting one another for the control of our music-halls, and we, the common crowd of Londoners, look on . . . It does not matter to us whether in the future the music-hall is to realise the ideals of the artistic or to satisfy the requirements of the moralists. We have lost it anyway. The two conflicting factions make up the conquering hordes of the upper and middle classes, and between them they have taken our music-halls from us . . .

We hear people talking in a very satisfied way about the wonderful improvement strides the music-hall has made in the past twenty years. If you come to look into it you will find that the improvement of the entertainment amounts to no more than the exclusion from the auditorium of the vulgar working-class population. The County Council, as soon as it came into existence, set itself to purify popular amusements, and as soon as it got well to work the big central music-halls were purified of their pit seats and the whole of the floor space was filled up with stalls at the popular price of seven and sixpence or half a guinea a-piece. The only place left for us was a gallery two miles high, and that at a price that made a big hole in the week's spending money.

As to our own little local music-halls, the purifying effect on them was to cause them to be floated with enormous capital and rebuilt as palaces and empires and hippodromes or under some other fancy names with such expense of marble and gilding and emergency exits that we could not get past the box-office. What passes for an evening's amusement at one of them is a seat on a back bench or in a high gallery for an hour and a half at one of the quick-turn twice nightlies. So the most we can expect to get is half an evening's amusement, and for fear we should get too fond of that they won't let us have any beer. So that if we want an occasional evening's complete enjoyment we have to spend half of it in a palace and half of it in a public-house, and neither of them quite satisfies us . . .

Out of the population of London there are five millions of us who habitually stop away from the music-halls. Believe me, it is not because we do not want to enjoy ourselves or have lost the capacity of enjoyment. We have not left the music-halls. The music-halls have left us . . .

The opposite view was put by an eminent Liberal polemicist, A. G. Gardiner: PILLARS OF SOCIETY *(1914)*

The other afternoon I went to a music-hall, one of those wonderful palaces that have sprung up in such abundance in the last twenty years, places where for a shilling or so you may sit on velvet, and pass through purple hanging, and be shown to your seat by magnificent persons in gold lace, and have tea brought to you between the turns by maidens, whose manners are as spotless as their caps. The music-hall of our youth was a thing of tinsel and orange peel, reeking with smoke and obscenity. There are people

who affect to deplore its disappearance. They exalt its freedom, its carelessness, its honest mirth. What they fail to recall is the fact of its filth. It was a noisome sewer, and one of the best signs of the times is that the sewer has been cleansed.

Not that all the critics were displeased with the general state of the music hall, and indeed many continued to praise it to the detriment of the legitimate theatre. Edward Gordon Craig: 'The Vitality of the Music Hall', THE MASK *(1911)*

The modern Theatre is worn out; it never was so worn out as it is today. The Music Hall, cherishing as it does so much creative talent of a somewhat exaggerated order is very much alive. Half, if not more, of the music hall 'turns' may be called creative. Madame Yvette Gullbert's performances are the finest examples of the living Music Hall. Madame Bernhardt, the most distinguished of those who have turned from the Theatre to the Music Hall, does no creative work of the kind, but the fact of so celebrated a performer appearing on the Music Hall stage must be accepted as the 'legitimate' Theatre's recognition of the force of what is known as the Variety stage.

Ironically the 1912 decision to legitimise music-hall performances of sketches may have been another cause of the decline: Beerbohm's 'nirvana' (see p 91) could not survive a forty-minute play.

Ragtime
Christopher Hassall describes the 1912 event that really slackened 'old-time' music hall's hold on the younger generation in his biography of RUPERT BROOKE *(1964)*

In . . . December . . . [*Hullo, Ragtime!*] opened at the London Hippodrome which nightly delivered an overwhelming assault of delightful and invigorating vulgarity noisy with brash splendours, magnificently

22 *Ethel Levey by W. K. Haselden.* Punch, *8 January 1913*

and a bracelet on her ankle . . . The American invasion of rag-time was a social event which Brooke welcomed as a sign of the times, Morris, Wilde, Shaw, Wells, G. E. Moore and the Fabians, they were all like intellectual sappers who had undermined the drawing-room and the conservatory on the mezzanine floor, and now it only wanted Alexander's Rag-Time Band, played by the American Ragtime Octet, and coon-shouted by an Amazon to push over the whole caboodle. During the next few months Brooke saw it ten times.

Revues of all types attracted not only younger potential music-hall audiences, but also music-hall stars (eg George Robey)—especially during the Great War.

The Great War
The halls played a considerable part in whipping-up anti-German feeling both during, and before, hostilities.
THE LETTERS OF RUPERT BROOKE (*1968*)

12 August 1914 'I've just been to . . . the Coliseum. It was pretty full. Miss Cecilia Loftus was imitating somebody I saw infinite years ago—Elsie Janis—in her imitation of a prehistoric figure called Frank Tinney. God! how far away it all seemed . . . Then a dreadful cinematograph reproduction of a hand drawing patriotic things—Harry Furniss it was—funny pictures of a soldier and a sailor (at the time, I suppose, dying in Belgium); a caricature of the Kaiser, greeted with a few perfunctory faint hisses. Nearly everyone sat silent. Then a scribbled message was thrown; 'War declared with Austria. 11.9.' There was a volley of quick low handclapping—more a signal of recognition than anything else. Then we dispersed into Trafalgar Square and bought midnight war editions . . . All these days I have not been so near tears. There was such tragedy and such dignity, in the people . . .

unashamed, in perfect accord with that element of animal violence which had been quietly stirring under the elegance of late Edwardian society . . . If ever the anti-Victorian intellectual has made a principle of irreverence, here it was in a popular cascade not sung exactly, but 'coon shouted', as the term was, by Ethel Levey, a woman of barbarous vigour with cropped hair under a wagging osprey, hobble skirt,

It is well known that when the soldiers marched off to glory they were inspired by music-hall songs—often adapted for their own purposes as John Brophy and Eric Partridge record in 'The Long Trail'. Thus Sub-Lieutenant Rupert Brooke and his men—the 2nd Naval Brigade—embarked for France behind a band playing music-hall tunes including 'Hullo Who's Your Lady Friend'. In 1916 Siegfried Sassoon expressed the growing disillusion with the halls' jolly propaganda, and the patriotic fervour they engendered from the safety of 'Blighty', in a bitter poem whose sentiments were echoed by an increasing number of soldiers during the last years of the war

23 *Harry Tate at a recruiting drive organised by Horatio Bottomly, Trafalgar Square, London, August 1915*

BLIGHTERS

The House is crammed; tier beyond tier they grin

And cackle at the Show, while prancing ranks
Of harlots shrill the chorus, drunk with din;
'We're sure the Kaiser loves the dear old Tanks!'

I'd like to see a Tank come down the stalls,
Lurching to rag-time tunes, or 'Home, sweet Home',—
And there'd be no more jokes in music-halls
To mock the riddled corpses round Bapaume.

Not surprisingly, therefore, many soldiers on leave, and their relations at home, turned to the cinema, especially as among the fare offered were the incredibly spectacular D. W. Griffith films: 'Birth of a Nation'

55

24 *Eli Hudson entertaining the troops 'somewhere in France' during World War I—possibly with his big hit 'You're the Sunshine of My Smile'*

(*1914*), *'Intolerance' (1916). The first comedy feature —'Tillie's Punctured Romance'—had been released in 1914, with the wildly popular Charlie Chaplin presenting British music-hall comedy at its most polished, and far more accessibly and cheaply than the halls themselves could now manage. The cinema was so successful that it was attracting condemnation from such bodies as the National Council of Public Morals. It set up a cinema commission of inquiry which published a* REPORT *in 1917. In this the chairman of the London Branch of the Cinematograph Exhibitors Association maintained, that*

The cheapness of this form of entertainment, has created what is really a new type of audience. Over half of the visitors to the picture theatres occupy seats to the value of threepence or less. In the main,

the vast majority of picture house patrons were not in the habit of attending any other places of amusement. The picture-house is emphatically the poor man's theatre.

The cinema also pleased because the performers, as well as the experiences, were new. A decade earlier Alfred Butt had told Percy Burton in an interview, 'How a Variety Theatre Is Run', in the STRAND MAGAZINE, *May 1909 that English artistes failed to follow French and American examples in inventing and developing new 'business'. English artistes were doing their turns to death.*

Like Butt's Palace, the Coliseum, however, managed to attract the crowds by presenting the best artistes from all branches of the theatre and all over the world. But generally the art of British music hall was moribund, the halls neglected, and audiences grew older and sparser. For the war and the subsequent 'flu epidemic had particularly affected those classes from which potential music-hall patrons had been drawn. *761,203 British servicemen were killed in the 1914-18 war. In addition 170,000, mainly young adults, died in the 'flu epidemic that ravaged Britain between July 1918 and May 1919. It was not surprising, therefore, that those young people remaining after 1918 should turn to something brighter, gayer, newer to distract their attention from the grim prospects before, and around, them.*

Jazz

It was the astute Albert de Courville (he had presented 'Hullo, Ragtime!') who produced the right thing at the right time: The Original Dixieland Jazz Band. 'Jazz' bands of sorts had been appearing in Britain since 1913, most were probably 'Ragtime' bands renamed to take into account the latest craze in the United States. But the ODJB was the first major American band to appear in the United Kingdom—although enthusiasts and servicemen knew its gramophone records well.

De Courville added it to the cast of his already jazz-orientated revue 'Joy Bells'. It opened on the 7 April; on 3 April it performed at a press conference. THE ERA, *9 April 1919*

The Original Dixie Land Jazz Band which arrived in London last week, and is now one of the many attractions in 'Joy Bells', gave a private performance between the afternoon and the evening shows. The bandsmen are white men from New Orleans, and the instruments on which they operate with such enthusiasm are a piano, cornet, clarinet, trombone, and trap-drum, the last named having an especially busy

25 *The Original Dixieland Jazz Band on the set for Phyllis Bedells' 'Bird Cage' ballet at the Hippodrome during the special performance for the press. Left to right: Nick La Rocca (cornet and leader), J. Russell Robinson (piano), Emil Christian (trombone), Tony Spargo (drums and kazoo), Larry Shields (clarinet) is standing behind piano*

time. A saucepan and a bowler hat were also used as adjuncts to the brass instruments in some of the selections, which included 'Tiger Rag' and 'The Barnyard Blues', and other exhilerating numbers. A clever and wonderfully agile speciality dancer [Johnnie Dale] is a member of the combination, the expert instrumentalists of which also proved their ability in 'straight' stuff and accompanying. The Dixie Land Jazzers are sure to be a big success.

They were, but the use of 'is' in the first sentence illustrates one of the dangers of a journalist writing about a performance before the event. For by the 9th the band had ceased to be part of 'Joy Bells'. Its star— George Robey—had been incensed over the fact that the band has 'stolen' what had previously been 'his' show. The theatre had been packed with American servicemen—on leave in London—whose enthusiasm had been contagious. There is no comprehensive contemporary account of the incident. H. O. Brunn: THE STORY OF THE ORIGINAL DIXIELAND JAZZ BAND (1961)

The fever spread through the theatre until every last man and woman was on his feet, shouting and clapping in a manner peculiarly un-British . . . when the curtain came down, George Robey . . . approached de Courville in a seething rage and served his ultimatum: Robey or the jazz band would have to go . . .

The band went, but was booked into the Palladium immediately, repeated its success, played a season at the newly-opened Hammersmith Palais de Danse, before embarking on a year's tour of the provinces which firmly established the dance-halls it played at as the new centres of urban entertainment. It also established jazz as the music of Youth, and ensured that it was not the passing craze sermonisers (both in and out of pulpits) considered it to be. The exact nature of Robey's complaint is not recorded for the rest of the 'Joy Bells'

cast even did not know why the band suddenly disappeared. [*Phyllis Bedells in conversation with Brian Rust, July 1972.*]

TOWN TOPICS, *12 April, had a topical explanation for the withdrawal, and also demonstrated that 'jazz' was basically a re-packaging of Victorian music-hall fare in a different form for a different audience*

The Dixieland Jazz Band appeared in 'Joy Bells' at the Hippodrome last Monday, but since has been withdrawn, presumably on account of the ubiquitous complaint, influenza. On the occasion of their performance, they gave us a demonstration of undiluted jazz, and it must be admitted, despite all that has been thought and said to the contrary, there was a certain charm in the mournful refrains, dramatically broken by cheery jingles and a miscellany of noises such as one generally hears 'off'.

Broadcasting

On 5 June 1920 Vesta Tilley made her farewell appearance and simultaneously the Westinghouse Company established the world's first broadcasting station in East Pittsburgh. Civil War swept Ireland. In 1921, 2,100,000 were unemployed in Britain. On 14 February 1922 the Marconi Company presented Britain's first entertainment broadcast; and on Easter Sunday, Herbert Austin took the road for the first time in the prototype Austin 7—cheap motoring and sprawling suburbs were on their way. On 29 July, Will Hay became the first major performer to 'broadcast'. It was a Marconi event, but, on 18 October, the British Broadcasting Company was formed, and on 14 November it commenced its public service. It was not surprising that Marie Lloyd's death on 7 October was seen by many as a symbolic event. Significantly the BBC's first variety show (30 January 1923) was 'Veterans of Variety'. Several other variety shows were given, and live broadcasts were made from theatres, but it is reported in the minutes of the BBC's Board of Governors'

MONOTYPE ATHLETIC CLUB FETE, HORLEY.
+ *Southwark Pageant*

FORECAST OF APPOLLO THEATRE "LISTENING IN".

6 - 6.30

(1)   Mr. Will Hay, Principal Comedian.   × *boy*
      " *School - Scene* "
Miss Clare + mr. nller   *accomp. by mr. Darewski.*
(2)   Miss M'Leta Dolores and Mr. Will Hay.
            Duet "Boy and Girl."
                   also " You never know".
all accompanied
      (3) *by* Mr. Herman Darewski, Piano.
            mr. miller - tenor

(4)   Miss Clarence Clare - Mr. Richard Neller
            Duet.

      Announced by mr Burrows.

26 *The entry in the Marconi programme file for Will Hay's pioneering variety broadcast. The programme was transmitted by land-line from the Marconi studios in the Strand and broadcast 'over a great part of England' as well as to the crowds at the fête*

meeting on 13 June 1923 that entertainment interests had decided that no facilities should be given to broadcasting. But to little avail. Broadcasting caught on even without major stars (it made its own), more and more halls either became cinemas, theatres or empty shells. However, only the performers and public lost, the theatre owners, and shareholders could not. For although the introduction of an Entertainment Tax in 1916—a tax not on profit but on turnover—meant that a small working surplus could be compulsorily converted into a loss by the Government, and managers made economies wherever possible, ultimately theatre owners and shareholders could not lose completely, as the introduction of Keith, MacAllister's BLUE BOOK *(1920) clearly showed*

The Entertainment industry has enjoyed an unparal-leled period of prosperity during the last four or five years, and up to the end of 1919 the general receipts have been in excess of any previous year . . . There has not unnaturally been an accompanying heavy increase in expenses, and the latter feature is one claiming direct attention now that the spending power of the public is showing signs of exhaustion. The immediate outlook is not very promising, and unless expenses can be cut down in proportion to any falling-off in receipts many under-takings must experience a considerable curtailment of profits.

However, in recent years theatrical and music hall management has vastly improved, and control of most of the larger companies has passed into the hands of competent business men.

Perhaps the surest way to prevent expenses growing unwieldy is by concentration of management. Already we have seen amalgamation of no mean importance, and this feature is likely to become more pronounced in the near future.

From the investment point of view, a good deal more can be said in favour of . . . music hall shares than ever was the case a few years ago. Generally speaking, the principal companies are now in a sound position . . . while a point which has not received the consideration it deserves is the enormous appreciation in the main asset ranking as security for the shareholder, namely, bricks and mortar.

The exact cause of the decline and death of music hall can never be firmly identified, even if it could be agreed that it did decline and die. For even in the 1830s the death of tavern halls had been reported. Benjamin Disraeli, SYBIL *(1845)*

'Well, what has Saturday to do with us?' said Caroline 'for neither Dandy Mick nor you can take us to the Temple, or any other genteel place, since they are all shut, from the Corn Laws, or some other cause . . .'

CHAPTER FIVE

THE STARS

It is obvious that without performers music hall would be impossible, for unlike plays which can be effective in print if necessary, the sketches and songs used on the halls depended entirely on the manner in which they were put over. Of course a good sketch or song could carry a poor performer along, or boost an accomplished performer to greater heights; but it should be remembered that though the singers and the comedians are the best-documented, the full range of 'variety' acts were presented in music halls throughout the nineteenth century. Where did the performers come from? Virtually anywhere. Who enabled them to appear? Managers, publicists and agents. For all these three played as large a part in building up the images and reputations of music-hall stars in the 'great days' as their equivalents did in Hollywood, and still do in all branches of show-business. H. G. Hibbert: FIFTY YEARS OF A LONDONER'S LIFE (1916)

It would be hard to estimate the direct and indirect obligation of the modern music hall, and of individual professors thereof, to his [Hugh Didcott] prescience and skill.

He was not the first agent—that distinction belongs to Ambrose Maynard, whose successor was Didcott's immediate predecessor, Charles Roberts . . . Didcott certainly endowed music hall agency with style and commercial system, and remained throughout his life its most picturesque figure. He has taken performers from soldiers' sing-songs, from Margate sands, from East End music halls, from penny gaffs —I could append great names to all these instances, but naturally I refrain. He has bestowed upon these 'discoveries' attractive descriptions, dressed them presentably, provided them with pocket money, selected songs for them and strenuously rehearsed them. Of a world-famous serio-comic singer, whom he admired prodigiously, his despair was that 'one might spend a hundred guineas on a gown for the —— and still she wouldn't clean her nails'.

Stars were publicised in the usual way: posters, especially 'personal' posters provided by the performers themselves for display in the towns they were visiting; press campaigns; song-plugging, personalised song sheets and song-collections advertised in the newspapers and music shops, and played incessantly on barrel-organs, and increasingly after 1900 on gramophone records. There were appearances at social events. A certain style had to be kept up in the streets on the way to engagements. William Holland provided George Leybourne (1842-84) who specialised in 'man-about-town' songs, including 'Champagne Charlie', with a carriage and four to drive to halls in a manner befitting his stage persona.

Maud Allan

The power of publicity is emphasised by the fantastic success achieved by the Canadian dancer Maud Allan (1883-1953) at the Palace Theatre in 1908 with her 'Dance of Salome'. Hibbert

It is safe to say that had Maud Allan's performance been casually introduced to the Palace programme it would have had short shrift. Instead it was managed with exquisite showmanship by Alfred Butt, with the assistance of the late Augustus Moore. For years Moore had professed the belief that an insidious and insistent journalist could make the London public form any opinion he chose as to the merit of a performance. He put his theories into careful practice with Maud Allan. The result was that for a year London, high and low, swarmed . . . to admire and applaud an artist of whom it had never heard before . . . Mr. Butt's first step was to issue invitations to a private performance. So aristocratic an audience has never filled a music hall, save at the command of royalty, as that which filled the Palace that afternoon in 1908. What persons of such high rank had applauded, should any common creature dare criticise?

Moore's part was the preparation of a pamphlet, insiduously circulated—and forming nine-tenths of the newspaper notices next day. Some critics ingenuously adopted its style and sentiment as their own. Some modestly placed inverted commas to choice extracts. Some interpolated a word or two of

27 *A personal poster (c1910) of the type artistes had to supply managers with upon their arrival at a hall*

deprecation. But in one form or another Moore's insinuated itself to every breakfast-table in London next day . . . And the Maud Allan boom began, and continued, as no boom did before in the history of the variety stage.

Albert Chevalier

Chevalier (1861-1923) was an ex-character actor reluctantly transformed into a 'coster' singer, who with

KEY TO "POPULARITY,"

Depicting Well-known Artistes of the Vaudeville Stage.

28 *'Popularity'. A vast oil-painting completed between 1901 and 1903 by Walter H. Lambert who appeared on the halls as Lydia Dreams in a female impersonation act. In addition to 226 recognisable portraits of leading performers it includes a self-portrait (177) and portraits of the artist's family (226–9). The setting is 'Poverty Corner' on the Waterloo Road, where unemployed artistes assembled outside the many agents' offices in the area. The 'Old Vic' Theatre is just out of the picture on the right. Note use of the word 'vaudeville' in the heading to the key. (Size of original 13 ft x 5 ft 6 in)*

1 Paul Cinquevalli	78 Jock Bennett	155 Harry Pleon
2 Dan Kelly	79 Charlie Martell	156 Harry Freeman
3 Griff	80 Herbert Darnley	157 Tom Leamore
4 Allen and Hart	81 Geo. Le Brunn	158 Charles Seel
5 Tom Morris	82 Little Ganty	159 Sam Poluski
6 T. Morris	83 Vene Clements	160 Ada Cerito
7 Harry Nation	84 Carrie Laurie	161 Tom Bass
8 S. Ethardo	85 Marie Kendall	162 Frank Folloy
9 Tom Vine	86 Daisy James	163 Will Poluski
10 Bros. Donaldson	87 Percy Delevine	164 George Mozart
11	88 Harry Delevine	165 Paul Martinetti
12 Willie Benn	89 Lottie Lennox	166 Alec Hurley
13 Richie Tom	90 Vosper	167 Pat Raffety
14 James Riley	91 Billie Barlow	168 Arthur Leonard
15 Arthur Harland	92 George Grey	169 Alice Lloyd
16 Albert Rollinson	93 Musical Korries	170 Eugene Stratton
17 Joe Gee (Burnells)	94 The late Bessie Wentworth	171 George Robey
18 The late Pat Feeney	95 Miss Korrie	172 Jimmie Hall
19 Jimmie Campbell	96 Sam Glenroy	173 Bill Horne
20 Albert and Edmunds	97 Charlie Fraser	174 George Le Clercq
21 Pimple	98 Jeff Vendome	175 Chris Horne
22 Dan Leno	99 Mrs Charlie Fraser	176 Charlie Fontaine
23 Nellie Wilson	100 Grell and Gray	177 Lydia Dreams
24 Arthur Forrest	101 Alice Maydue	178 Jessie Preston
25 Nellie Richards	102 Jerry Driscoll	179 Georgina Preston
26 John Lawson	103 Bob Allinson	180 H. Missouri
27 Horace White	104 Dean Tribune	181 J. Sothern
28 Tom Collins	105 Jean Seul	182 Will Oliver
29 Lilly English	106 Ernest Rees	183 Fred Mc'Naughton
30 George Booker	107 Douglas Stuart	184 Tom Mc'Naughton
31 Fred Griffiths	108 Walter Norman	185 Joe Elvin
32 Albert Le Fre	109 Edna Cragge	186 Jack Lotto
33 Joe Griffiths	110 Ida Heath	187 Wal Pink
34 Harry Champion	111 F. Ayling	188 Miss Bella) Bella and
35 Harry Anderson	112 H. Harris	189 Mr Bijou) Bijou
36 Harry Blake (2 B's)	113	190 Kate Carney
37 Bob Leonard	114 Fish and Warren	191 James Fawn
38 Jack Camp	115 The late Jolly John Nash	192 Marie Lloyd
39 Ford and Hanson	116 The late Geo. Leybourne	193 T. E. Dunville
40 Fred Millis	117 Will Evans	194 Katie Lawrence
41 Hanson	118 May Henderson	195 Vesta Victoria
42 Capt. Slingsby	119 Tom Maxwell	196 Mr Leamy
43 Tom McKay	120 Virginia Francis	197
44 Sisters Levy	121 The late Charles Laurie	198 Ara and Vora
45	122 Jack Lambert	199 Fannie Leslie
46 The late Mrs Florador	123 The late Ada Lundberg	200 J. O'Gorman
47 Floradon	124 Tom Holmes	201 Michael Nolan
48 Harry Lauder	125 Kate Paradise	202 Joe Tennyson
49 Paul Courtenay	126 Wilkie Bard	203 Horace Wheatley
50 Frank Coyne	127 M'Chalk	204 Walter Munroe
51 Tom Wootwall	128 The late Charles Godfrey	205 Johnny Dwyer
52 Nat Clifford	129 Jack Selbini	206 Pat Carey
53 Dutch Daly	130 James Norrie	207 Harry Ford
54 Reid Pinaud	131 Charlie Cornish	208 Vesta Tilley
55 Chirgwin	132 Fred Russell	209 The late Bessie Bonehill
56 Walter Stockwell	133 Florrie Ford	210 R. G. Knowles
57	134 Bransby Williams	211 Arthur Lloyd
58 Two Harvey Boys	135 J. W. Cragg	212 Charles Coborn
59 Rumbo Austin	136 Alexandra Dagmar	213 Gus Elen
60 Charles Tempest	137 The late Tom White	214 Jenny Hill
61 Johnny Dane	138 Lieut. Travis	215 Peggy Pryde
62 Arthur Pearl	139 Cliff Ryland	216 Albert Chevalier
63 Jack Rowley	140 Barney Armstrong	217 Arthur Rigby
64 Bros. Passmore	141 Charlie Alexander	218 Papa Brown
65	142 Harry Randall	219 Little Tich
66 The late Bessie Bellwood	143 Herbert Campbell	220 Carrie Lorrie's Juveniles
67 Harry Lester	144 The late Tom O'Brien	221
68 Charlie Edwards	145 Jack Collinson	222 Character
69 Con Fredericks	146 G. W. Hunter	223 Mr Smith's Dog
70 Charles Morton Esq	147 Vento	224 Dandy George's Dog Rosie
71 Marie Loftus	148 Eddy Hanlon	225 T. Beck
72 Cissie Loftus	149 Bob Hanlon	226 Artist's late Wife
73 Tom Branford	150 Teddy Bale	227 Child of Artist
74 Charlie Clark	151 George Lashwood	228 Child of Artist
75 Tom Costello	152 Harriet Vernon	229 Child of Artist
76 Clarke (Clarke & Glennie)	153 Jennie Valmore	230 Will Crackles
77 Gus Garrick	154 Harry Gee	231 Jack Rich

MACDERMOTTS NEW SONG,

DEAR OLD PALS.

Dear old pals, jolly old pals!
Clinging together in all sorts of weather;
Dear old pals, jolly old pals,
Give me the friendship of dear old pals.

WRITTEN & COMPOSED BY
G. W. HUNT,
SUNG WITH IMMENSE SUCCESS
BY
G. H. MACDERMOTT.
LONDON HOPWOOD & CREW, 42, NEW BOND ST W.

29 *A cover by Alfred Concanen—the most prolific and accomplished of the Victorian lithographers who worked in this field—for one of the most typical music-hall songs of its period*

30 A 'street-ballad' type of cover of the 1890s, listing not only songs connected with Leno but also other evocative titles of the period

Mc. GLENNON'S AUTHORISED EDITION.   PRICE ONE PENNY.

THE GREAT
DAN LENO'S
SONG BOOK.

CONTENTS.

MY SWEET FACE
THE DOCTOR
RECRUITING ✳ THE JAP
THE SHOP-WALKER. | THE WAITER.
MARY ANN'S REFUSED ME

THE MIDNIGHT MARCH

Don't You Believe It

SUSI-AN-I-OH

The SANDWICH MAN

You get there just the same

THE HIRING SYSTEM

THE POSTMAN'S RAT-TAT

SWEET CHIMING BELLS

ALICE GREY

Rocked in the Cradle of the Deep

I couldn't help but laugh

THE LOST CHORD

BARNEY, TAKE ME HOME

MINSTREL BOY

The ship that carries me home

Take you home again, Kathleen

SOLDIER AND A MAN

Nancy, or Still True Blue

ROBIN, ADAIR

SHADOW AND SUNLIGHT

ALL THROUGH A LITTLE
PIECE OF BACON

DETECTIVE CAMERA

The Grass Widower ; or, She's
Going Out of Town

NORINE MAUREEN

Home, Home, Sweet Home

THE MUFFIN MAN

Spare the old Mud Cabin

MY OLD MAN

WOMAN'S IN IT

As Hot as I can Make it

DEAR OLD MIKE

The Railway Guard

Her Mother's at the Bottom of it all

NEVER MORE

DAN LENO.

Published at McGlennon's "Song Book Office." 47 & 49, Spear Street, Manchester.
Wholesale Agents—Abel Heywood & Son, Oldham Street, Manchester.
London Office:—223, Wa'erloo Road, S.E.

31 *Alfred Butt. Drawing by H.C.Q.,* Vanity Fair, *21 December 1910, also showing Maud Allan—and the head of John the Baptist. Butt was knighted in 1919 'For generous and useful contributions to War Charities and War Work. Served in Ministry of Food 1917-1918'*

the aid of an astute manager (Charles Ingle) made the idea of music hall acceptable to the middle classes, and female upper classes, through extensive seasons of afternoon concerts at the Queen's Hall, London, and in provincial concert-halls. Also he gave recitals in fashionable drawing-rooms, even though he revealed in

66

'The Coster in Society' THE GRAPHIC 29 November 1892 that

They are an abiding terror to me. Whenever I have accepted an engagement, I always feel, as the time approached, that it is for my sins. You see, it's one thing to face a music-hall audience which knows you and likes you (and if it is at the Mogul, is going to sing part of your songs for you), but quite another to stand up in the chilling air of a drawing-room and tell people, who wonder who on earth you are and what on earth a coster is like, that 'yn't the sort o' bloke to go abaht and tear your 'air'.

He essayed many other roles on the music-hall stage, but his 'coster' songs were the most admired. There had been many stage cockneys before Chevalier for example, in 'Tom and Jerry', and adaptations of Dickens' novels. Sam Cowell (1820-66) with 'Villikins and His Dinah'; The Great Vance [Alfred Peck Stevens] (1839-88) with 'The Chickaleary Cove'; Jenny Hill (1851-96) with ''Arry' had all represented certain aspects of the Cockney character on the halls themselves. There had been innumerable 'real' cockneys in East London Halls, but it was Chevalier who developed a fully-rounded theatrical type or 'mask' for the extraordinary individual figure—the coster. Chevalier also developed stage-business still in use eighty years later. W. R. Titterton: FROM THEATRE TO MUSIC HALL (1912)

The verse finishes, the coster turns, toys with his hat, in one quick movement the billycock has struck ten attitudes, and then the shoulders are squared, the elbows stick out, and the foot leaps forward before the straightened leg into that inimitable coster stride.

As the surname implies Chevalier was not wholly English. Max Beerbohm, 'Yvette Guilbert and Albert Chevalier', SATURDAY REVIEW, *23 June 1892*

He has Italian as well as French blood in his veins. And this admixture accounts for the vivacity of face and figure that surprised us so much in the early nineties . . . [But] despite his vivacity, he has never picked up the knack of ease and quickness . . . He makes a dozen gestures, a dozen grimaces, when one would be ample. He suits the action to the word so insistently that every word, almost, has an action all to himself.

There was another aspect of Chevalier's performance which many thought noteworthy. THE DIARIES OF LEWIS CARROLL *edited by Roger Lanceyln Green (1953)*

His chief merit seems to be the earnestness with which he throws himself into the work. The songs (mostly his own writings) were quite inoffensive, and

32 *'Mr. Albert Chevalier singing one of his coster songs in a West-End drawing-room'*

very funny. I am very glad to be able to think that his influence, on public taste, is towards refinement and purity.

But as many deplored his purifying influence as praised it, and the deplorers usually preferred Gus Elen (1862-1940) maintaining that he was a genuine working-class 'coster' rather than a middle-class character actor. In an interview reprinted in VARIETY STARS *edited by A. J. Park and Charles Douglas Stuart (1895) Elen, however, revealed that he was only acting the part of a coster in true Stanislavskian manner*

I don't confine myself, however, in my attempts at

MISS LOTTIE COLLINS
AT HOME.

"Moy song is jast immense,
Sam soy it's got now sense,
Sam soy th'y down't know whence
It kime, but twown't gow hence.
I down't mean now offence,
But whoile I gily dence
An' medly jemp an' prence,
It brings me lots of pence.

(*Spoken.*)—" Pence, indeed—shillin's an' pounds ! to soy nothin' of benk-nowtes ! !

Ta-ra-ra-BOOM-de-ay."

33 Caricature of Lottie Collins from 'Footlights' 1895

realism to the mere dressing of the part, but endeavour to identify myself absolutely with the character reproduced.

Lottie Collins

Whether popular singers and comedians are 'actors' or not still confuses the public, and critics, and often the performers themselves. With dancers the problem is not quite so difficult. Obviously they are performing in a manner very different from 'real' life behaviour. Lottie Collins's (1866-1910), fame rested almost entirely on the frenzied dance she used to accompany her 'de-oderised' version of a bump-and-grind song from the bordellos of New Orleans. Frank Rutter described her chanting her barbaric hymn 'Ta-ra-ra-Boom-de-aye' as if in a trance to an audience as still and serious as if it had been in a church. She was important also as one of the first British popular entertainers whose act was seen as politically significant by certain witnesses not wholly present with the intention of glimpsing forbidden areas of female anatomy. Holbrook Jackson: THE EIGHTEEN NINETIES *(1913)*

Our new-found freedom seemed to find just the expression it needed in the abandoned nonsense chorus 'Tar-ra-ra-boom-de-ay!' which lit at the red skirts of Lottie Collins, spread like a dancing flame through the land obsessing the minds of young and old, gay and sedate, until it became a veritable song-pest, provoking satires even upon itself in the music halls of its origin. No song ever took a people in quite the same way; from 1892 to 1896 it affected the country like an epidemic; and during those years it would seem to have been the absurd *ca ira* of a generation bent upon kicking over the traces.

Symbolically, Lottie Collins collapsed and died of a heart attack only four days before Edward VII's death marked the end of an era. Although one of the king's favourites, she did not (and could not) receive a royal command.

Dan Leno

Edward VII could and did ask Dan Leno [George Galvin] (1860-1904) to receive a royal command—the first non-circus comedian to be so honoured in the post-Georgian period. Max Beerbohm's valedictory essay with its strikingly poetic opening sentences 'So little and frail a lantern could not harbour so big a frame. Dan Leno was more of a spirit than a man.' is often reprinted but THE TIMES' *obituary, 1 November 1904, gives an equally vivid impression of his art and technique*

Mr. Leno had not only a rich fund of comedy in his own quaint face and person, he had that far rarer gift—the intelligence to make use of it. Whether at Drury Lane or the Pavilion, he was always the same, yet always different. At Drury Lane he played many old women [in pantomimes] . . . but Mother Goose was quite different from Widow Twankey perhaps his most famous part, and both were other than the Mrs. Kelly who delighted thousands at the Pavilion. In the same way, the shop-walker (with the famous talk on eggs) was quite other than the huntsman or the beefeater. And yet each had the same face, the same smile, the same twinkling eyes, and the same twinkling feet. Mr. Leno was, in fact, a close student and an able exponent of character. He had imagination. He was not content to trade solely on what nature had given him. He could hardly walk, and certainly never dance, without raising a smile; but he had a hundred different ways of walking and dancing, each appropriate to the person he was representing . . . and, though it is no secret that he did not invent all his quips himself, he gave them all new point . . .

Twelve years earlier 'The Spectator' (probably Arthur Symons) had diagnosed the simultaneous reasons for Leno's success, his insanity, his mental decline, and

DAN LENO'S COMIC Journal

½

No. 4. Vol. I.
WEEK ENDING
March 19, 1898.

"ONE TOUCH OF LENO MAKES THE WHOLE WORLD GRIN."

DANIEL'S DARLING TAKES UP THE EDITORIAL REINS.

EVERY TUESDAY.

My Dear Friends,—It was not merely the pride of wealth that made me have the above photo taken. We do have fish for dinner, and we've got two clocks and a money-box and some cockroaches in our back kitchen. I am proud of my home, and I admit it. How nice it is for a man to come in after a hard day's work and find a tasty little dinner ready—a sausage and mashed and a bit of Gorgonzola, or something like that! A man's wife is his helpmeet; but that doesn't always mean that she can cook meat, or fish either. Sometimes she's better at editing a paper. Oh, crumbs! It's worse than wicked.

All rights preserved.

Dan Leno

34 *Leno was the first real person to be immortalised in a comic* the heart attack that caused his death, in a review of the bill 'At the Middlesex' in THE STAR, *10 September 1892*

His expenditure of brain and nerve and muscle on a single 'turn' is tremendous; he realises that (not invariably false) definition of genius as an infinite capacity for taking pains.

Little Tich

Little Tich [Harry Relph] (1868-1928) was as popular and highly considered as Leno in his day, but since his death the type of comedian (the similar-sized, or even smaller and more obviously deformed, slightly manic dwarf engaged as a fool in royal and aristocratic households, and displayed to the populace in circuses and sideshows) of which he was the last great example has fallen into complete disrepute. Nowadays many would side with 'The Spectator' who observed in 'The Star' on 9 September 1893 that 'Personally, I do not take much pleasure in the contortions of this grotesque homuncule, this footlight Quasimodo . . .' He was a very small man somewhere between four feet and four feet six inches tall, and painfully aware always of the extra finger on each hand. He undoubtedly exaggerated his smallness by having his costumes carefully cut, and by appearing with larger than average accomplices. But*

35 *Cigarette-cards were another much-sought-after form of publicity*

Little Tich & Miss Ffolyette·

Ogden's Guinea Gold Cigarettes.

36 *Song-cover illustrating not only Little Tich's Big Boots and his jester antecedents, but also his slightly manic stare and (even more unusually) his deformity*

he did not trade on his size by playing small people, or schoolboys, in fact he seemed to ignore his size altogether, as the best account of his act emphasises. Paul Nash: OUTLINE (*1949*)

As we took our seats, the orchestra struck up one of those brisk and merry tunes which are inseparable from Tich's public personality—a very different personality from his private character which was rather grave and inclined to studiousness. . . . He was able to be funny in so many ways—in appearance . . . a face rather like Punch's but more intelligent, agile as a mongoose, but capable of the most absurd and alarming tumbles and gestures, and then a voice of many modulations from shrill girlish piping to guttural innuendoes and sibilant 'double entendres'. But his strangest most compelling asset were his feet. These I think were normal in themselves, but were habitually inserted into the most monstrous boots, long, narrow and flat, so long that he could bow from the boots and lean over at almost an acute angle from his heels . . . The scene tonight was a familiar one . . . On the right-hand wing, a corner house with an area and a grating . . . Suddenly he sees the grating. At once the gay, innocent comic becomes a mischievous little monster, all leers and terrible chuckles . . . his little stick held casually behind his back somehow begins to look like a little dog's tail which begins to wag with pleasure. The audience is not slow to get all these signs and they laugh and hoot and whistle rude whistles . . . Tich becomes tremendously animated and does a wonderful little dance, slapping his boots together in midair. He throws up his hat and in his ecstasy throws away his little stick. This aberration suddenly halts the whole show. The band stops: while Tich tries to move towards recovering his hat but hesitates and turns to the direction of his stick, and then changes his mind again, and so on, until he is demented with worry. However, the band creeps in *sotto voce* and

this seems to encourage him to pick up his stick firmly. But as he stoops to gather up his hat, the toe of his long boot pushes the hat ahead, sometimes it goes only just out of reach, sometimes it positively jumps like a frog. Then suddenly Tich either kicks it, or hits it in a miraculous way so that it spins into the air and he catches it on his head. This is the signal for the band to open up again. Tich resumes his dance and amid a storm of applause the turn is over.

Marie Lloyd

Reformers and moralists had complained about the offensiveness of male, low comedians for many years. But none of them had been able to make as much profitable 'advertising copy' out of the criticism as Marie Lloyd [Matilda Wood] (1870-1922) was able to make out of the adverse criticisms she received. NEW YORK TELEGRAPH, *14 November 1897 even carried an article over her name in which 'Miss Marie Lloyd criticizes her own risqué songs'.*

I might as well say right here that my songs are not blue—at least not half as blue as they are painted . . . The trouble is that the people are looking for blue, and I can't help it . . . if they want to turn and twist my meanings . . . I don't make them blue. It's the people . . .

Arguments about whether she sang rude songs or not still rage in music-hall circles. For she above all others is seen as the epitome of the real spirit of British music hall of the pre-1914 period. As far as her posthumous reputation is concerned, she had the good fortune to be the subject of a famous essay by T. S. Eliot, in itself an important landmark in the intellectual consideration of popular entertainment from a sociological and political angle.

Until well into her thirties (like Mary Pickford), both she and her audiences preferred to see her in songs

37 *Marie Lloyd dressed as a schoolgirl for her controversial song 'Johnnie Jones'*

characterising various aspects of young, and even schoolgirl, life. H. G. Hibbert explained

There was a naive innocence in her songs of those days. She made her first advance towards the suggestiveness encouraged in her later life with 'Keep Off The Grass', 'Then You Wink The Other Eye' . . . [she] displayed a rather rare tact in her accommodation of her art to her years. She was only 52 when she died. She was so young when she first impressed herself on the popular imagination that there was a disposition to believe she was much older . . . The first song in which she admitted the passing of the years was entitled. 'You're a thing of

the past, old dear.' It was at once recognised that in the dashing serio-comic singer we had a character actress of rare insight . . . It was a little amusing to note the reluctance with which Marie Lloyd gave herself up to the art of 'low comedy'. She would alternate a conventional 'serio' song, 'The Cosmopolitan Girl', with such 'rough stuff', . . . as 'One of the Ruins Cromwell Knocked About'. The Cromwell, let it be explained, figured on the signboard of a public house: the ruins were its too-frequent frequenters. It was in this character of a drunken woman, staggering on the stage of the Edmonton Empire, that Marie Lloyd fell. The

38 *Marie Lloyd in her Golders Green bedroom, 1922*

audience shrieked with laughter at the realism of the scene. It has often laughed at such an incident, from Peg Woffington's seizure onwards. The stricken actress was carried home to die.

Her death had been hastened by a decision to accept Stoll's invitation to appear in an Old Time Music Hall show at the Alhambra when in less than full health. She was an outspoken woman off-stage, as an early cinema technician—Albany Ward—recorded for THE HISTORY OF THE BRITISH FILM 1896-1906 *(1948) by Rachel Low and Roger Manvell*

At that time on the Music Halls we showed from behind through a transparent screen, viz. a fine calico screen which was thoroughly damped with water and glycerine . . . I well remember . . . getting fearfully ticked off by Marie Lloyd, who was the Turn following us as we wetted the stage rather badly, to which she took very strong and forcible objection, particularly as far as language was concerned.

W. R. Titterton gave the essential ingredients of her stage persona in FROM THEATRE TO MUSIC HALL *'happy, healthy, boisterous, magnetic coster-girl . . . splendid frankness . . . hearty laughter . . . chic, electric, alluring walk . . . in hobble skirt . . . quick inevitable twists and turns of body and hands . . . flashing eyes . . . flashing teeth, and the rosebud, pouting, impudent mouth!'*
'Spectator' put the antipathetic view in THE STAR *14 October 1893*

She typifies, I suppose, the 'knowing' female, the sophisticated young person for whom life has no secrets. But imperturbable self-confidence and a trick of winking at every other word strike me as rather inadequate compensations for a shrill voice and a toe which is neither light nor fantastic. But in the music halls it is, I believe, almost impious to

THE CALL BOY'S GIRLS.
No. 39.—Miss Marie Lloyd.

39 *Devastating caricature of Marie Lloyd by Alfred Bryan*

question the talent of Miss Marie Lloyd . . .

The tremendous crowds at her funeral amply demonstrated the extraordinary hold she had over her public who had followed closely the well-known vicissitudes of both her public and private life, and possibly benefitted from her largesse. An interview in 'The Sketch' 25 December 1895 reported that she was paying nightly for one hundred and fifty beds for the homeless and destitute of 'Darker London'.
H. G. Hibbert concluded his obituary by saying 'it is not cruel to say that she dies opportunely . . . the music hall is on the eve of a crisis.'

40 *Marie Lloyd's funeral*, The Times, *13 October 1922*

George Robey

One of the crises was the growing age of the leading stars. Marie Lloyd, Little Tich, Albert Chevalier, George Robey and Vesta Tilley were all in their fifties in 1920. Like Marie Lloyd, Chevalier died opportunely, Little Tich died soon after but George Robey [George Edward Wade] (1869-1954) carried on working right up to his death, even though his powers steadily declined after 1922. He was the exact antithesis of Marie Lloyd. She was, as Eliot observed, of the unsophisticated common people, and this was the image she projected both off- and on-stage. Robey on-stage was sophisticatedly common, but off-stage he took care to emphasise that he derived from lower middle-class stock, and publicised a definitely un-common life-style. This encompassed strong anti-clericalism; Freemasonry; Conservatism; active participation in cricket and soccer; love of classical music, serious literature and antique objets d'art; a strongly censorious attitude to anything new eg jazz; and a tendency to make public pronouncements on

41 *George Robey with his first wife (Ethel Hayden), his daughter Eileen, and his son, who as Sir Edward Robey was a Metropolitan Magistrate from 1954-72. A post-card portrait publicising Robey's lower middle-class 'family' life-style*

these matters—attitudes and preferences which did not always engender appreciation within the profession. He claimed also that he had been educated at Jesus College, Cambridge but inspection of the records there proves this to be just a piece of publicity. On stage all was forgiven, as he was the complete master of every aspect of music-hall technique. In an article on Robey in IMMOMENT

Mr. Robey's patter is everything now, and yet he says, altogether, wonderfully little; first a word, and then he seems to detect some misplaced laugh in the audience, checks, bridles up, passes in pantomime from tantrum to tantrum, the gusts and squalls of temper coming and going in him visibly. You may call the topics outworn and trivial, the mere words insignificant, the humour metallic, rasping, or worse, but the art, within its limits, is not to be surpassed in its gleaming, elliptical terseness, the volumes it speaks in some instants, its suddenness, fire and zest.

Harry Lauder

For his services to war charities Robey only received the CBE in 1919 whereas Harry Lauder [Hugh MacLennan] (1870-1950) received a knighthood, probably because his humour was less 'rude' than Robey's. In addition Lauder had served the cause of Empire well throughout his career, he was possibly even more popular in America, Canada and Australia among expatriate Scotsmen, who found his sentimental songs and sketches matched perfectly their rose-tinged memories of home. Of all the music-hall stars he was the most astute businessman, and it is this 'canny' aspect that has enraged many Scots keen to protect the dignity of the Scottish character from what they consider Lauderesque caricatures. There are many stories of his financial acumen. In his account of Movietone James L. Limbacher recalled how at the first test film made by Lauder, he sang his 'Roamin' in the Gloamin'' and to be sure that the film would not be shown commercially . . . stopped in the middle of the song and inserted the phrase, 'This is a test'. On 8 April 1910 he wrote to J. Howie Milligan whose songs (eg 'Roamin' in the Gloamin'') were published invariably as Lauder's own work 'Enclosed find cheque for £2. Give me a receipt for £10—this is for reference to enquiries as to how much I pay for my

42 *Harry Lauder with the symbol of his fame*

material, and it doesn't pay to tell every Tom, Dick and Harry your private biz.'

He could, however, be much more generous with personal, and charitable dealings—if he felt the occasion demanded it. W. R. Titterton summed up the attraction his act held

He struts round the stage like a bantam, smiling broadly, quirking his head to the rhythm of the music . . . He is beautifully poised, he treads as if on air, his big limbs move with the daintiness of a prima ballerina. The lilt of the music runs through his body and breaks into radiance in his universal smile . . . You feel happy and comfortable, and don't know why . . . You see the slow deliberate thoughts puckering his brow, you mark the deliberate gesture and the halting speech . . . And yet—one longs for the exuberance. And when the exuberance comes it carries us away, and leaves us with a pleasant taste in the mouth and a sense of the sun having shone upon us.

The comparison with a conventicle congregation was apt as Lauder was one of the first music-hall stars to appear in a church. DAILY MAIL, *24 January 1913*

Mr. Harry Lauder occupied the pulpit yesterday afternoon at Anerley Congregational Church, South London, and addressed a crowded men's meeting on the treatment of pit ponies. Many were unable to obtain admittance, and late-comers had to stand or sit on camp stools in the aisles. After an enthusiastic reception the comedian and ex-miner earned further applause by singing 'Annie Laurie' . . . After his address . . . Mr. Lauder received another ovation when he sang, 'Rocked in the Cradle of the Deep'.

Vesta Tilley

Unlike Robey and Lauder—who both continued to perform until the end of their lives—Vesta Tilley [Matilda Powles] (1864-1952) chose to retire in 1922. 'Vesta Tilley's Farewell', the DAILY TELEGRAPH, *7 June 1922*

It was a memorable occasion at the Coliseum, and the vast auditorium, packed to its utmost, could have been filled again and again by thousands of the artist's admirers. Enthusiasm reached a high level when the orchestra, by way of introduction to the 'star turn', gave a selection of songs recalling the earlier successes of the lady whose popularity, long and lasting though it has been, has never stood higher than it does at the leave-taking. Miss Tilley included among her farewell

43 *Vesta Tilley in a punt on the Thames with her husband Sir Walter de Frece*

numbers some of the songs that caught the fancy of her admirers many years ago, and each was rendered with all her accustomed art, that evoked rapturous cheers. The curtain fell amid a scene of great enthusiasm, only to rise again, when Miss Tilley advanced to the footlights and became the recipient of countless baskets of flowers and bouquets, which transformed the stage into a garden of roses. An affecting little incident was witnessed when Miss Ellen Terry came forward, and placing her arm round Miss Tilley with an affectionate gesture said: 'I am not going to make a speech. I could not do it. I could not say enough of what I think of this wonderful little lady—I mean this wonderful little gentleman. (Laughter). I know this, that if I do begin to speak I shall never leave off. Miss Tilley does not know what she has done for England. She made us laugh when, God knows, we needed to laugh. Now she deserves a crown. I have not got a crown about me—(touching her pocket)—but I will present her with a palm.' The great actress then placed in Miss Tilley's hands a wreath of palm leaves. A further tribute of admiration took the form of an album containing the signatures of nearly a million wellwishers . . .

Undoubtedly both she, and her husband realised that it would be impossible to present her act as a living force rather than a mere curiosity in the post-war world. Increased sophistication, and a wider knowledge of Freudian psychology, would have led to unsympathetic analysis of her act which was solely that of a male impersonator. There were many male impersonators but she was the foremost as she paid such close attention to detail. 'She even walked with her feet apart just like a man.' Thus Laura Knight pinpointed in 'Oil Paint and Grease Paint' (1936), the keynote of her characterisation. For it was her close study of the different walks men adopt for different jobs that placed her so far ahead of her contemporaries, and, of course, completely beyond emulation by any of her successors. Unfortunately she had perfected her art at such an early age, and had maintained her leading position for so long, that few critics bothered to record the exact details of her performances. Titterton: FROM THEATRE TO MUSIC HALL

The band is playing a merry dancing chorus you know. A ripple of applause grows to thunder and dies away in the gallery . . . And the orchestra plays

44 *Vesta Tilley in immaculate Edwardian man's suit*

the chorus through again, for Vesta Tilley, artful fellow! loves to keep us waiting and expectant. There is a low buzz of a bell, the conductor bends to his orchestra, the chorus starts again, and a dapper young man in an exquisite purple holiday costume strolls from the wings leaning on his bending cane. He comes to the centre of the footlights, and poses with crossed legs and staring monocle, the features deliciously quizzical and inane. A perfect picture . . . the picture speaks and the illusion is piquantly broken, or, rather, the optical illusion continues, only there is another person present—the woman artist who unfolds the tale . . . Every gesture is right; every tone is right—striking the delicate chord between irony and burlesque . . . How sure the singer is! How despotically she rules over her audience—dallies with the rhythm, draws it out, pauses in mid-gesture, the hand in the air, the monocle nearing the eye—pauses perilously long you get uneasy . . .

In addition to providing an extraordinarily evocative picture of Vesta Tilley as 'Burlington Bertie', W. R. Titterton also delineates many of the characteristics of the performances of all the outstanding music-hall stars of her day.

The Performance

Obviously the outstanding post-1922 stars depended for their hold on their audiences upon the old techniques. The predecessors of Vesta Tilley had gained their places in a similar fashion. The nineteenth-century stars did not just spring from nowhere. Like the form of theatre in which they appeared, the types of artist they represented had existed for centuries, but their acts had not been recorded in such detail as their contemporaries' on the 'legitimate' stage. Even the phrase 'star' was in use (in the modern sense) in the middle of the eighteenth century and there were 'chairmen' in all but name. George Alexander Stevens. THE ADVENTURES OF A SPECULIST (*1788*)

We went to COMUS'S COURT, as they called it, one JACK SPEED'S White Horse, Fetter Lane . . . When we had taken our seats, and I had once or twice looked round the room, and examined the many persons who were placed on each side of two long tables, I could not observe that their eyes discovered the least symptoms of jollity: on the contrary, their faces were mere blanks, and they seemed most earnestly looking about as if they wanted something

they could not describe . . .

I told this to my conductor, who whispered to me to have a little patience; that the Stars did not appear soon that night, but that I should see them shine, or at least twinkle, by and by; that the company I now saw did not meet to make one another merry, but to be made merry by others . . .

Now 'silence! silence!' was bawled out by almost every person in the room, and every body stood up on the President's rising, who had been a very wealthy tradesman formerly, but had ruined himself by attending upon such meetings as these, merely to get the name of a CLEVER FELLOW.

After most deliberately hitting three strokes upon the table with his hammer, he began with telling the company, 'that he had a toast or two to propose, after which Mr. GRUNTER should either give them the organ, the broomstick, a French-horn tune, or a song first; but that if he might take the liberty of speaking before a set of such gentlemen of merit as he saw there, he presumed that if Mr. GRUNTER opened with a song, it would be most agreeable'.

But he did not find what to many was the mainspring of Victorian and Edwardian music hall—the band. W. L. George: LONDON MOSAIC (*1921*)

You can't drowse in a music-hall: from the moment when the conductor, in his elaborately luxurious and irredeemably faulty dress suit, addresses his first and infinitely disabused bow to the audience, to the time when he calls upon the band to produce the smallest possible scrap of 'God Save the King', and hurries out loyalty on the wings of ragtime, there is no flagging . . . The main thing is the band, the harsh, rapid band, that never stops, that plays anything, providing it is the thing of the day, with all the regularity and indifference of the typewriter. From it gush patriotism, comedy or sentiment, and all three burst forth with their full headline value. There is no tickling of big drums; when the drum is banged you know it; nor is there measure in the sigh of the oboe, for the music-hall paints not in wash-greens and grays; scarlet, black, white and electric-blue are its gamut.

The overall effect was, therefore, continuous noise from both the stage and orchestra pit, and the auditorium. The audibility of individual performers varied, but as audiences were often engaged in other activities, knew the songs by heart, or frequently sang the songs with or *instead of, the performers, this was not always noticed.* THE JOURNALS OF ARNOLD BENNETT 1896-1910 (*1932*)

May 8th 1896 . . . I think I never saw the Empire so full, Yvette [Guilbert] wore a gown of bluish green flowered silk, and the unchangeable black gloves. To the back of the pit, where I stood, her voice came as if from an immense distance, attenuated, but clear and crisp.

James Ritchie: DAYS AND NIGHTS IN LONDON (*1880*) for my shilling I could see little, and hear less.

CHAPTER SIX

THE AUDIENCE
AND THE ATMOSPHERE

Even stars, however, would be nothing without audiences and although styles of entertainment may have varied throughout the ages, basically the types of entertainment and the audiences have not. Richard Doyle: BIRD'S EYE VIEWS OF SOCIETY (*1864*)

A great want must surely have been met when promoters and managers of the People's amusements first conceived the happy thought of combining singing and tumbling, and eating and drinking, and smoking . . . to be able to sit, with a little table before one, with, for instance, a bottle of beer upon it, to have one eye turned upon an acrobat, the other gazing affectionately at the drink, a cigar hanging lazily from the mouth . . . considering each song, dance, or other performance with an impartial look of languid contentment, a hazy, sleepy, stolid, stupid, sense of smoke, and drink, and general enjoyment.

The smoke, however, did not come entirely from

cigars. *George Bernard Shaw:* THE WORLD, *24 January 1894*

Now when the ordinary products of respiration are added to the smoke of hundreds of cigarettes and of the hundreds of holes which the discarded ends of them are burning in the rather stale carpets . . .

Alcohol
Whereas smoking was allowed in legitimate theatres, drinking in the auditorium was not and it was this facility that was the main attraction (or disadvantage) of the music halls. In fact many considered that the main purpose of the halls was the encouragement of drinking. The Hon S. C. B. Ponsonby in the Select Committee on Theatrical Licences and Regulations. Report (1866) regarded the entertainment as only an accessory to the sale of drink at the Canterbury Music Hall, whereas at a theatre, drink was only an accessory to the play. James Ewing Ritchie in DAYS AND NIGHTS

IN LONDON (*1880*) *expressed his conviction that music halls were primarily places in which people were licensed to drink, with the music present only as an after-thought on the part of the management.*

Thomas Wright: SOME HABITS AND CUSTOMS OF THE WORKING CLASS BY A JOURNEYMAN ENGINEER (*1867*)

The refreshments supplied in these halls, however, are generally moderately good, but at the same time more than moderately dear, while the waiters, who, in accordance with the usage of these establishments, have to be pecuniarily 'remembered' each time that they refill your glass or bring you the most trifling article haunt you in an oppressive and vampirish manner if you venture to linger over your drink; and all things considered, it is not too much to say that, notwithstanding the comparatively low prices of admission . . . music-halls are about the dearest places of amusement that a working man can frequent.

CHURCH REFORMER, *June 1892, defended the halls*

45 *The pictorial side of the programme at the Palace Theatre, London, 2 September 1912 shows clearly the type of clientele Butt was seeking at that time. The bill consisted of fifteen acts but was dominated by Winifred Emery in a sketch, Gaby Deslys in a Musical Comedietta and the Palace Bioscope*

As a matter of fact just as much is spent on alcoholic liquors by the audience of a theatre as by that of a hall. The difference only lies in where they spend it. At a hall there are no passes outside, and, therefore, all money for drink is spent inside. At the theatres on the other hand, in the lengthy intervals between the acts, a great proportion of the audience pass outside and obtain refreshment at the neighbouring public houses.

Nevertheless it would seem that music halls were instrumental in maintaining the consumption of beer in particular at a time when the depression and the temperance movement might have been expected to have an adverse effect on sales. The fact that the workers

83

THE
CONVIVIAL
SONG BOOK.

CONTENTS:

JOHN BARLEYCORN.
The Queen, God Bless Her.
Champagne Song.
Cheer, Boys, Cheer.

Old King Cole.
I Wish You All Good Health.
Now, Boys, what's it going to be?
Come, Send Round the Wine.

The Leather Bottell.
One Bumper at Parting.
Drink to Her Who Long.
Oh, Bring Me Wine.

Mynheer Vandunck.
Auld Lang Syne (Though Full of Beer.)
We are Four Jolly Good Fellows

GIVE ME A GRIP
To Your Girl My Girl.
All In A Row.
The-Rowdy-Dowdy-Boys.

DEAR OLD PALS.
We're All Right.
Fill The Glass.
Let's Be Jolly While We May

One More Glass Before We're Parting
The Glasses Sparkle on the Board.
The Merry Little Fat Grey Man.
Come, Thou Monarch of the Vine

THE LITTLE BROWN JUG.

THE GOOD RHINE WINE
Hi! Boys. Hi! Boys.
Hi-Tiddley-Hi-Ti.
La-Diddily-Idily.

Simon the Cellarer
We've Drank from the same Canteen. [Corner.
Bless the Little Pub round the

Down Among the Dead Men
A Little More Cider.
Push About the Bottle, Boys
When Your Glass is Empty.

Drinking, Drinking, Drinking
Whiskey.
The Cruiskeen Lawn.
Sweethearts and Wives.

OF YOUR HAND.
Give It A Name.
Oddfellows.
We Walked Home.

DRINK, BOYS
Who Deeply Drinks of Wine.
Go Fetch to Me a Pint of Wine
The Maids of Merry England

A King must lead a happy life.
Many Happy Returns of the Day
Take a Bumper and Try.
Taste, oh, Taste This Spicy Wine

MY FRIEND AND PITCHER

Published at McGlennon's "Song Book Office. 47 & 49. Spear street. Manchester.
Wholesale Agents Abel Heywood & Son Oldham Street. Manchester
London Office. 223 Waterloo Road. S.E.

46 *Cover of song-book listing the titles of some of the pro-drink songs 'plugged' incessantly during the 1870s and 1880s when the Temperance Movement was particularly active*

continued to drink Tory beer was a disappointment to ardent Socialists. THE JOURNALS OF ARNOLD BENNETT

1896-1910 (*1932*)

25 March 1908. The news of the triumph of beer in the Peckham election this morning really did depress me . . . I read in the *Daily Mail* this morning that, when the news of the triumph of beer got into the music-halls last night there were scenes of wild enthusiasm . . .

The Spectators

To many of course the basic idea of theatre (with its hypocritical pretence, painted faces etc) was anathema. Charles Booth pinpointed another aspect which displeased those who viewed Work as a Religion. LIFE AND LABOUR OF THE LONDON POOR. 3RD SERIES, RELIGIOUS INFLUENCES, Vol 3: THE CITY OF LONDON AND THE WEST END (*1902*)

Among the poor people living in the Notting Dale area drink does not seem to account sufficiently for the extra expenditure perhaps pleasure-seeking does —such as visits to the music hall in winter, and constant day trips and outings in summer. With these people work never stands in the way of pleasure.

This piece of sociological evidence serves to offset much of the reportage about the grim conditions and long working hours prevalent in the nineteenth century. They could be grim and they were long. Mass Observation: THE PUB AND THE PEOPLE (*1943; repr 1970*)

Shorter working hours may appear, on one hand, to give more time for drinking, and on the other, to produce less inclination to drink as a reaction from fatigue. But while today in Worktown the cotton workers spend less time than ever before in the mills, the actual intensity of the work is very much higher.

Today when most urban thoroughfares are comprehensively illuminated, the effect a brightly lit and noisy

public house or music hall had on its immediate environment cannot be appreciated fully. And, although it is about a music saloon, an article on 'Labour and the Poor: the Manufacturing Districts' . . ., Letter VII probably by Henry Mayhew in the MORNING CHRONICLE 8 November 1849, catches fully the atmosphere that must have existed outside most local halls until the 1900s

The London-road, [Manchester] on Saturday night, has very much the appearance of Tottenham-court-road, in the metropolis; at the same period of the week. It is full of cheap shops, devoted to the sale of ordinary household matters. Stalls, covered and uncovered, heaped over with still coarser and cheaper wares, abound. Gas flares and blazes amid the joints in the butchers' open shops. Faintly burning candles, enclosed in greasy paper lanterns, cast their dim and

47 *'London Sketches—at a Music Hall' by J. D. Linton, 1873. A mixed audience—including a woman smoking—and not one person watching the performer*

tallowy influence over tables slimy with cheap fish, or costermongers' barrows littered with cabbages or apples. The gin-shops are in full feather—their swinging doors never hang a moment still. Itinerant bands blow and bang their loudest; organ boys grind monotonously; ballad singers or flying stationers make roaring proclamations of their wares . . . Boys and girls shout and laugh, and disappear into the taverns together. Careful housewifes—often attended by their husbands, dutifully carrying the baby—bargain hard with the butchers for a halfpenny off in the pound. In a cheap draper's shop, a committee of young women will be examining into the merits of a quenting . . . [promenades] do so because they think it sounds fast and impresses others with the idea that they are gay livers . . . and persuade themselves that the men they see around them are 'real swells' . . . [they] seem to have no suspicion that the men they see are little better than themselves. And yet . . . the full-dressed men to be found in such a place comprise the loafers of the West End, the sons of the big shop keepers, the smaller members of the Stock Exchange, the livery-stable keepers, the West-End wine-bar proprietors, and all those men, who daily brought into contact with gentlemen, fancy they have only to assume the feathers to become counterparts of the bird . . . Another fault . . . is that, in addition to the time-wasting movements encouraged at all such places, they add the development of snobbery and shoddy gentility . . .

The Bird
Music-hall audiences were not afraid of expressing their opinions. W. L. George: LONDON MOSAIC *(1921)*

48 *The audience in the gallery at the Metropolitan, Edgware Road, London c1902*

dress which one of them has determined to buy; while, in an underground pie-shop, a select party of juveniles will be regaling themselves upon musty pasties of fat pork. The pawnbroker is busy, for pledges are being rapidly redeemed . . .

A bright lamp over an open door points out the entrance to lovers of harmony and beer. Here there is a check-taker, helped, and no doubt superintended, by a policeman, who will not allow drunken people to pass.

Although there were family parties (particularly in the smaller local halls) young men dominated the audiences. TEMPTED LONDON: YOUNG MEN *(1888)*

The clerks and others who . . . drift into fre-

If within one minute of his appearance the performer has not got his laugh he will probably not get it at all. If he is famous, and if his turn is not too bad, nothing worse will happen than the administration of the frozen lemon. It is rather tragic, feeling the lemon come. You feel the audience leap up towards the performer, for it is always ready to give him his chance, even if he is unknown; then, in a minute or so, you feel the audience drop away from him, you are aware that he is not being listened to, for people begin to talk, to flutter with their programmes, and perhaps some one may hum an irrelevant air. The wretched performer knows it. If you are sitting in the first row of the stalls you see anxiety come over his face. He begins to shout or to dance rather wildly; he knows that he is not getting across; he tries to attract attention as a cockatoo if he cannot do so as an eagle. Then some one laughs derisively, and there

49 Cover of an album of the 1870s which included songs on the full range of popular music-hall topics of the day. Some of the songs are still closely related to folk and street ballads eg 'Walter Cresses' and 'The Sewing-up Machine'

is something hideous in that laughter; it makes one think of the thumb-down attitude in the Roman circus. The curtain drops in the middle of something that is half hum and half silence. That is the lemon.

It is only in extreme cases that the audience manifests disapproval. Indeed, it is an audience full of good-natured contempt, and if the lemon is taken it willingly passes on to the next turn; as a rule, the lemon is taken by the management, who ring down the curtain on the first song and do not let the performer come on again. But if the performer does come on again, and strives to recapture lost ground, the audience will give him thirty seconds to do it; if he fails, the hum grows angry as that of a swarm of bees. There is more derisive laughter; a few yells come from the gallery; a general uproar develops from the hum. You discern cries: 'I want to go 'ome' . . . 'Take me back to mother' . . . Opponents reply as loudly: 'Shut up! chuck him out!' But the voices resume in more and more sepulchral tones: 'I want to go 'ome', while others join the rag for the rag's sake, and some stentor high above roars: 'Shut yer face, dear, I see yer Christmas dinner'. And then everybody cries: 'Chuck him out!' while the performer sings louder and louder and the band makes still more desperate efforts to drown his song. Then a large portion of the audience rise to their feet and bellow enmity until the curtain goes down. That is the scarlet bird, and I have not often seen it on the wing.

No, there is no mercy in the music-hall audience. For it is an honest audience, and is, therefore, capable of every brutality. Also, everybody has paid for his seat. Nobody there can afford to waste that small payment. They must get their money's worth . . .

Writers and the Music Hall
The audience was one of the main attractions, either to those who just wanted to be part of it, or to those who

wanted to observe it. THE JOURNALS OF ARNOLD BENNETT 1911-1921 (*1932*)

April 21st [1911]. London Palace Theatre. Pavlova dancing the dying swan. Feather falls off her dress. Two silent Englishmen. One says, 'Moulting' . . .

Arthur Symons: 'A Spanish Music-Hall', written c1900 CITIES AND SEA COASTS AND ISLANDS (*1919*)

In a music-hall the audience is part of the performance. The audience in a theatre, besides being in itself less amusing, is on its best behaviour . . . [but] Here we have a tragic comedy in the box yonder, a farce in the third row of the stalls, a scene from a ballet in the promenade. The fascination of these private performances is irresistible; and they are so constantly changing, so full of surprises, so mysterious and so clear.

Admiration of, and personal involvement in, popular entertainment, by intellectuals, writers and artists has a longer tradition on the continent (especially France) than in Britain. It was French example that led Symons and George Moore to treat the halls as symbolic of their revolt against middle-class respectability. 'The music-hall is a protest against the villa, the circulating library, the club . . .' Many, however, (at all levels of society) used the halls as 'clubs' where they might be certain of meeting friends and colleagues. Following the French tradition, some English painters and poets, such as Arthur Symons, used the halls and their inhabitants as subject matter for their work. Although he never dealt with the halls in his poetry, and only occasionally with them in his fiction, the poet most popularly associated with the halls is Rudyard Kipling. His poems were popular fare (either declaimed as dramatic monologues or sung) with music-hall audiences; and they had in fact been inspired by them. SOMETHING OF MYSELF (*1937*)

Meantime, I had found me quarters in Villiers Street, Strand . . . from my desk I could look out of my window through the fan-light of Gatti's Music-Hall entrance, across the street, almost on to its stage . . . fourpence, which included a pewter of beer or porter, was the price of admission to Gatti's.

It was here, in the company of an elderly but upright barmaid . . . that I listened to the observed and compelling songs of the Lion and Mammoth Comiques, and the shriller strains—but equally 'observed'—of the Bessies and Bellas, whom I could hear arguing beneath my window with their cab-drivers, as they sped from Hall to Hall. One lady sometimes delighted us with viva-voce versions of —'what 'as just 'appened to me outside 'ere, if you'll believe it.' Then she would plunge into brilliant improvisations. Oh, we believed! Many of us had, perhaps, taken part in the tail of that argument at the doors, ere she stormed in.

Those monologues I could never hope to rival, but the smoke, the roar, and the good-fellowship of relaxed humanity at Gatti's 'set' the scene for a certain sort of song. The Private Soldier in India I thought I knew fairly well. His English brother (in the Guards mostly) sat and sang at my elbow any night I chose; and, for Greek chorus, I had the comments of my barmaid . . . The outcome was the first of some verses called Barrack-Room Ballads.

Kipling's dictum. 'Old music-hall ditties . . . supply a gap in the national history; and people haven't yet realised how much they had to do with the national life' has frequently been reproduced in the many sociological studies of popular songs to appear since he wrote it in 1934. But the same point had been made over sixty years before by the Rev H. R. Haweis who was also a pioneer commentator on the artificially short life of popular songs. MUSIC AND MORALS (1871)

Music is thus approaching in England to what it has ever been in Germany—a running commentary upon all life . . . Our street ballads last but from year to year, almost from month to month; they are constantly being replaced, not by songs that enrich the national stock, but by songs whose chief object seems to be to extinguish their predecessors, and when they have accomplished this, die themselves.

The British painter of music-hall subjects to come nearest his French counterparts (eg Degas and Toulouse-Lautrec) was Walter Richard Sickert. In a letter he explained

I was intensely impressed by the pictorial beauty of the scene, created by the coincidence of a number of fortuitous elements of form and colour. A graceful girl leaning forward from the stage, to accentuate the refrain of one of the sentimental ballads so dear to the frequenters of the halls, evoked a spontaneous movement of sympathy and attention in an audience whose sombre tones threw into more brilliant relief the animated movement of the singer, bathed as she was in a ray of green limelight from the centre of the roof, and from below in the yellow radiance of the footlights . . .

It is obvious that Sickert really loved the halls, but the attitude of their most famous intellectual critic was always objective, although his reports were always intensely evocative. Max Beerbohm 'At the Tivoli', SATURDAY REVIEW, *3 December 1898*

Here, in these very stalls, I would often sit with some coaeval in statu pupillari. Lordly aloof, both of us, from the joyous vulgarity of our environment, we would talk in undertones about Hesiod and Fra Angelico, about the lyric element in Marcus Aureleus and the ethics of apostasy as illustrated by the Oxford Movement. Now and again, in the pauses of our conversation we would rest our eyes upon the stage

50 'A Bioscope in a music hall'. Oil-painting by W. R. Sickert c1900. An extremely vivid study of a subject perfectly suited to the artist's preoccupation, in his music-hall paintings, with the contrast between the bright stage and the silhouettes of the audience

and listen to a verse or two of some song about a mother-in-law or an upstairs lodger, and then one of us would turn to the other, saying, 'Yes! I see your point about poor Newman, but . . .' or 'I cannot admit that there is any real distinction between primitive art and . . .' Though our intellects may not have been so monstrous fine as we pretended, we were quite honest in so far as neither of us could have snatched any surreptitious pleasure in the entertainment as such. We came simply that we might bask in the glow of our own superiority—superiority not only to the guffawing clowns and jades around us, but also to the cloistered pedascules who, no more exquisite than we in erudition, were not in touch with modern life and would have been scared like so many owls, in that garish temple of modernity, a Music Hall, wherein we, on the other hand, were able to

sit without blinking. Were we, after all, so very absurd?

Robert Emmons gave the accepted, rather sentimental, view of the reasons why the ordinary person went to the halls, in the LIFE AND OPINIONS OF WALTER RICHARD SICKERT (*1941*)

The patrons were . . . the 'lads' of the district, the local bookie and his clients. To them the music hall . . . was an enchanted palace, where they could forget their troubles in a warm world of magic and romance.

Beerbohm, however, spotted the political implications of the entertainment (implications many would decry as biassed misunderstanding after the event) in 'At the Tivoli'

The aim of the Music Hall is, in fact, to cheer the lower classes up by showing them a life uglier and more sordid than your own. The mass of people, when it seeks pleasure, does not want to be elevated: it wants to laugh at something beneath its own level. Just as I used to go to the Music Halls that I might feel my superiority to the audience, so does the audience go that it may compare itself favourably with the debased rapscallions of the songs . . . the entertainments in Music Halls are the exact and joyous result of the public's own taste. 'Turn' by 'turn', these entertainments have grown up with reference to nothing but the public's own needs and aspirations. There is no compromise, no friction, between the form and the audience. The audience is the maker of the form, the form is the symbol of the audience. And thus Music Hall offers always a great chance to any student of humanity at large.

Sixty years later, Raymond Williams expressed similar thoughts in THE LONG REVOLUTION (*1961*)

The urban working class created in the Industrial Revolution found in these performers their most authentic voices . . . it is common to make a sentimental valuation of the music-halls as expressing the spirit of 'Old England' (which is nonsense in that what they expressed was not old) or as signs of a great cultural vitality.

John Osborne made such a claim in an introductory note to his play THE ENTERTAINER (*1957*)

The music hall is dying, and, with it, a significant part of England. Some of the heart of England has gone; something that once belonged to everyone, for this was truly a folk art.

Like so many others, Osborne ignores genuine modern manifestations of the music-hall aura—not usually to be found in 'Old-Time Music Hall' shows. 'Old-Time' music hall died in 1923; it is possible the modern

equivalents of the audiences, atmosphere and performances, are to be found at pop concerts rather than in variety theatres. Max Beerbohm. 'Music Halls of My Youth', THE LISTENER, *22 January 1943*

I had ceased to attend halls before the virus of 'Variety' had come creeping in . . . The magic had fled—the dear old magic of the unity—the monotony, if you will,—of song after song after song, good, bad, and indifferent, all fusing one with another and cumulatively instilling a sense of deep beatitude, a strange sweet foretaste of Nirvana . . .

That pop concerts (and television) do provide the modern equivalent of music hall is made clear if they are substituted for 'music-hall' in this passage from George Gamble: THE 'HALLS (*1899*)

From the music-hall come the melodies that fill the public mind; from the music-hall come the catchwords that fill the public mouth. But for the fecundity of the music-hall, how barren would be the land, how void the chit-chat of the drawing-rooms, the parlours, the sculleries! In what way, other than by apeing the latest contortion, could 'Arry make Arriet guffaw? In what way, other than by parrotising the latest witticism, could Edwin make Angelina giggle? And, in what way, other than by ambling through the latest skirt-dance, could Gwendolen captivate the soul of Algernon? How would the bean-feasters conceal their sadness, if there were no comic songs? How would the Bank-holiday makers conceal their boredom, if there were no waltz-refrains? And how would the urban and suburban classes and masses beguile the tedium of slow hours, and find an excuse for pausing in their 'life-work', if there were no barrel-organs to brinkerty-brankerty, crinkerty-crankerty, drinkerty-drankerty—and so on through a whole horrisonous alphabet of machine-made discord?

CHAPTER SEVEN

THE LAW AND
THE MUSIC HALL

Licensing and Censorship

Throughout most of the period under review, there was

a distinction between the music-halls within twenty miles of London and Westminster and those in the provinces . . . A music-hall within twenty miles of London or Westminster is any place to which the public are habitually admitted by the proprietor for the purposes of either hearing music or seeing or taking part in dancing or any like entertainment. Every such music-hall must be licensed under 25 Geo. II. c. 36 . . . and further if it is an actual building and situate within the metropolitan area, it must confirm to the structural conditions prescribed by the Metropolitan Board of Works . . . If the public are not admitted indiscriminately, it will not be within the statute . . .

W. N. M. Geary: THE LAW OF THEATRES AND MUSIC-HALLS . . . (*1885*). *Elsewhere music-hall licences*

were issued by licensing justices or local authorities under powers derived either from special local Acts or by adoption of Part IV of the Public Health Amendment Act 1890. The latter also enabled the licensing authority to attach conditions to licences. The attached conditions usually were intended to prohibit profanity, improper dress, striptease, or any poster or advertisement likely to be injurious to morality. This in spite of the fact that there was never any statutory censorship of music-hall material, in the sense that details of scripts, stage business or choreography had to be submitted in advance of presentation to any of these authorities, or even to the Lord Chamberlain. But while he did not seek to censor the contents of music-hall performances, the Lord Chamberlain did seek to ensure that stage-plays of any length were not presented in the halls. This ruling (under the Theatres Act, 1843) caused much wrangling both inside and outside courts, and widespread evasion of the ban.

A Select Committee on Theatrical Licences and

Regulations was established to examine this problem as early as 1866. Its REPORT (1866) *revealed that there were known to be twenty-eight music halls in London presenting theatrical entertainments without the correct licence, and noted also that in 1865 the Court of Common Pleas had upheld the decision that a 'Pepper's Ghost' performance was a 'play'. The owner of Day's Music Hall in Birmingham was convicted accordingly. In addition the Hon S. C. B. Ponsonby of the Lord Chancellor's Office observed that another*

point in litigation between the music-halls and the theatres is the interpretation of the words 'dancing, music, or other public entertainments of the like kind'. It is whether those words mean that the audience were to dance or whether they were to look at the dancing . . .

By 1900 the situation had got completely out of hand. Henry Arthur Jones: AN OPEN LETTER TO THE RIGHT HONOURABLE WINSTON CHURCHILL, MP (1910)

Throughout the kingdom there are, it is estimated, 150,000 illegal performances of stage-plays in music-halls every year, and the number is increasing . . .

In fact Charles Morton had successfully applied for a theatrical licence for the Philharmonic Music Hall, Islington in 1871. And so with this precedent it was not surprising that in spite of continued opposition from the legitimate stage and moralists, the halls' campaign against the ban was successful. T. H. S. Escott: ENGLAND ITS PEOPLE, POLICY AND PURSUITS (1870)

Free trade in theatres . . . has made room on the stage for . . . the crapulous buffooneries of the music-hall. Indeed, while the music-hall is a grade above the gin-shop, it is the curse of the stage. It vitiates and debases managers, actors, audiences alike. As a consequence, it is but too likely that were

the Act of Parliament for regulating theatres repealed the result would be, not the conversion of music-halls into theatres, but of theatres into music-halls.

The 1892 Select Committee on Theatres and Places of Entertainment had had, in spite of spirited objections from the leading actor and playwright of the day— Henry Irving and Arthur Wing Pinero—and other powerful figures from the legitimate stage, recommended in its REPORT (1892) *that*

there should be at least three classes of licences; one for theatres proper, where smoking and drinking would not be permitted in the auditorium; one for those music-halls which are now sometimes called Theatres of Varieties, and one for concert and dancing rooms . . . that in theatres of varieties it be made lawful, without the possession of a licence for stage plays, publicly to present ballet, ballet divertissement, or ballet of action, and those performances commonly called sketches, if the duration of each such performance shall not exceed forty minutes, and no more than six principal performers take part therein, and if there shall be an interval of at least thirty minutes between any two such sketches, and no two sketches performed on the same evening at such place of public entertainment shall have a connected plot . . .

This recommendation was acted upon in 1912. John Palmer: THE FUTURE OF THE THEATRE (1913)

People prophesied that, if the Lord Chamberlain allowed these little plays to be given in music halls, there was an end of the theatre. He was told that the music hall and the theatre were in competition; that the music hall licensed for music and dancing had many advantages over the theatre licensed only for stage plays; that signing a licence for the performance of a play at the Palace or the Tivoli would be signing the death-warrant of English drama. It is not possible here to tell the story in detail—how the music-hall proprietors asked for licences; how they were refused; how they defied the law; how they were sued by the 'legitimate' managers; how they made illegal compacts wherein it was agreed that prosecutions should not be brought so long as the plays were very short; how at last the Lord Chamberlain's hand was forced by the County Councils; and how in January 1912 he began to license stage plays as part of a variety programme . . . and that thereafter everything went on as before.

Especially after a summons brought by Harley Granville Barker against the New Tivoli Limited 'for presenting for hire alleged stage plays that had not been allowed by the Lord Chamberlain' had been dismissed. The case was heard at Bow Street Police Court on 16 April and 8 May 1912. The 'alleged stage plays' were an act by a ventriloquist (Johnson Clark) in which he carried on dialogue with a dummy not sitting on his knee, and Little Tich's Guardsman and Gamekeeper sketches. This was a test case for the type of entertainment possible in music halls, but no case established definitively what words and actions songs and sketches might contain. The Select Committee of 1892 had also re-affirmed a recommendation of the 1866 Committee

that the censorship of plays has worked satisfactorily, and that it is not desirable that it should be discontinued; on the contrary, that it should be extended as far as practicable to the performances in music-halls and other places of public entertainment.

But the Lord Chamberlain made no attempt to bring the halls in line with the theatres, presumably because enough powers were available under the local Acts to deal with objectionable matter, if it was thought necessary and possible. THE JOURNALS OF ARNOLD BENNETT 1896-1910 (1932)

January 2nd, 1910 . . . I couldn't see the legendary cleverness of the vulgarity of Marie Lloyd. She was very young and spry for a grandmother. All her songs were variations on the same theme of sexual naughtiness. No censor would ever pass them, and especially he wouldn't pass her winks and her silences . . .

Bennett was wrong as the local authority 'censors' had invariably 'passed' them, as in spite of their powers they had rarely brought charges against music-hall performers. George Bernard Shaw, 'The Shewing-up of Blanco Posnet', the preface (1909) in THE COMPLETE PREFACES OF BERNARD SHAW (1965)

Municipal control of the variety theatres (formally called music halls) has been very far from illiberal, except in one particular in which the Lord Chamberlain is equally illiberal. That particular is the assumption that a draped figure is decent and an undraped one indecent. It is useless to point to actual experience, which proves abundantly that naked or apparently naked figures, whether exhibited as living pictures, animated statuary, or in dance, are at their best not only innocent, but refining in their effect, whereas those . . . skirt dancers who have brought the peculiar aphrodisiac effect which is objected to to the highest pitch of efficiency wear twice as many petticoats as an ordinary woman does, and seldom exhibit more than their ankles.

Shaw also observed that the 'indecency' in the sketches and songs lay between the lines rather than in the lines themselves, but that it was not this factor, but the

practical impossibility that prevented the London County Council from attempting to apply a censorship of the Lord Chamberlain's pattern to the London music halls. A proposal to examine all entertainments before permitting their performance was actually made; and it was abandoned, not in the least as contrary to the liberty of the stage, but because the executive problem of how to do it at once reduced the proposal to absurdity. Even if the council devoted all its time to witnessing the rehearsals of variety performances, and putting each item to the vote . . . the work would still fall into arrear . . .

The only solutions he concluded would have been to attach an inspector of morals to each hall, or to close them altogether. Neither of his suggestions was adopted, but an increasing number of charges were brought against music halls for presenting lewd sketches. For example, in 1912, The Rev H. M. Ward (who had not seen the item himself) complained to the Lord Chamberlain about a play performed by Gaby Deslys and her company at the Palace. This sparked-off a nice little storm in a teacup. The headlines to the DAILY MAIL's coverage of the affair tell the story

THE LORD CHAMBERLAIN AND MLLE. GABY DESLYS. PROTEST TO THE PALACE THEATRE. MANAGER'S ACTION. NO CHANGE IN THE 'TURN'. 23 October 1913. MUSIC-HALL MORALS. CAMPAIGN OF THE BISHOPS. 'We expect the Public to back us up.' HOT REPLY BY MR. ALFRED BUTT. A 'DAILY MAIL' SPECIAL COMMISSIONER. SEX AND ART. AIMS OF THE BISHOP OF KENSINGTON. 11 November 1913. MUSIC-HALL MORALS. AN INCIDENT AT THE ALHAMBRA. The Church is strong enough to enforce its standard. 12 November 1913. MUSIC-HALL MORALS. THE FAMILY PARTY. DISCOMFITED MEN WITH DAUGHTERS. VISIT TO THE NEW MIDDLESEX. UNMISTAKABLE SNIGGER. ALL AGES AND SEXES. 'FRENCH VIVACITY.' THIRSTY IMITATORS. 13 November 1913. MUSIC-HALL MORALS. VISITS TO THE CHIEF PERFORMANCES.

SATISFACTORY VERDICT. CLEAN ENTERTAINMENTS FOR THE FAMILY. FEW DOUBTFUL 'TURNS'. 14 November 1913. MUSIC-HALL MORALS. A MAN WHO HISSED. ASSAULT BY PERFORMER. 21 November 1913.

On most aspects of the relationship between the performers and their employers the usual laws applied. But there were instances where the special nature of music-hall work was recognised. The Select Committee on Theatres and Places of Entertainment reproduced a programme from English's New Sebright Wholesome Amusement Temple in their REPORT (1892). It contained

Notice to Artistes.—In addition to the ordinary rules of this establishment, the following suggestions are to be observed:—No offensive allusions to be made to any Member of the Royal Family, Members of Parliament, German Princes, police authorities, or any member thereof, London County Council, or any member of that body; no allusion whatever to religion, or to any religious sect; no offensive allusions to the administration of law of the country.

Coarse jests and rough language to be particularly avoided.

It is the desire of the management to please the whole and give offence to no portion of the audience. Artistes would do well to assist in this object, and consider that many of the above topics are thoroughly worn out, and consequently become objectionable instead of entertaining.

Terms of Employment

The REPORT also reproduced artistes' contracts from the Middlesex, Collins' and the Royal Albert. All contained similar 'small-print', but the latter was the most comprehensive

1. No person other than performers or dressers

can be allowed behind the curtain or in the dressing rooms under any pretence whatever.

2. Artistes are not to stand in the passages behind the curtain, nor to interfere with the stage employees; must not make any observations upon the performance of other artistes or the orchestra, and smoking behind the curtain or in the dressing rooms, loud talking, singing, or other noise not directly connected with the performance, are strictly prohibited. No artiste shall address the audience except in the regular course of the performance; and any allusion to engagements at other establishments is absolutely forbidden. Any breach of this rule will entail the forfeiture of a night's salary.

3. No artiste shall perform at any other place of entertainment within one mile from the Royal Albert Music Hall, nor at any occasional concert, town hall, or institute, without the written consent of the management.

4. A proportionate reduction of salary will be made for every evening when the hall is closed by order of the public authorities, by accident, or any other cause.

5. Engagements to be void if the performance is objected to by the public authorities.

6. No comic or serio-comic song may be sung at this establishment without the written approval of the management, and a copy of every comic or serio-comic song intended to be sung by any artiste must be left with the management two days at least before such song is to be sung, and no variation will be permitted from the words so approved. Any artiste giving expression to anything obscene or vulgar in song, saying, or gesture, or of political, religious or local matters, will subject themselves to instant dismissal, and shall forfeit any salary that may be due for the current week.

7. Artistes must be in attendance at least ten minutes before the time named by the management for their appearance on the stage, and although any artistes may be put on ten minutes later than the specified time, they must, if required do the whole of their performance.

8. If any artiste is considered by the management incompetent to fulfil the duties of the engagement, such artiste will be subject to dismissal at the end of the performance, and the payment only of that night's salary.

9. The inability of any artiste to attend his or her duties must be communicated in writing to the management, and in case of illness must be accompanied by a medical certificate. The management shall not be bound to pay any salary during such absence, and should such absence exceed one week, the engagement may be cancelled at the option of the management.

10. All artistes agree to hold the management free from and against all loss, costs, damage, or other expenses, in the event of them singing or performing, without written permission, copyright music, words, or other performances.

11. All persons to attend rehearsal when required.

12. The proprietor reserves the right to prohibit any song, music, or performance.

13. The proprietor will not hold himself responsible for any article, wardrobe, or music left in the establishment.

14. Salaries will only be paid for actual services rendered.

15. Advertising matter for bill or specimens of posters, &c., to be forwarded ten days before commencing this engagement . . .

The barring clause in particular sparked-off the 1907 strike and the arbitrator made certain amendments *(see p 48)*.

CHAPTER EIGHT

FINANCE

Salaries

Theatre finance has always been a complicated business, and one about which there has been too little information. Various aspects have been illustrated already (eg p 48). The most notorious, however, has not: the vast sums earned by leading performers when compared to the wages of 'ordinary' workers or even the best-paid executives. 'Music-Hall Business', ST JAMES GAZETTE, 27 April 1892

Music-hall artists of good position earn very comfortable incomes. At a highclass West-end hall not one, out of the score or so that make up the programme, will be found to earn less than £10 a week, and most of them may be credited with considerably more—from £20 to £50 a week. In exceptional cases £60, £70, and even £100 a week represent the modest gains of these popular idols. It would hardly be fair to give more exact particulars. Her Majesty's Revenue Officers seem to have their eye on the profession . . .

Of course the large salaries are not all earned at one hall, but by appearing at several—possibly as many as six—every night. An artist of the second line will generally perform at three or four places nightly, receiving at each £10 or £12 a week; and one of the first rank will do the same at £20 or £25. The necessary expenses involved are considerable—there is the carriage, the dresser, the agent's commission, and so on . . .

As the writer suggests individual salaries are difficult to assess, but H. G. Hibbert quoted some weekly 'Salaries of Celebrities' in Chapter XX of FIFTY YEARS OF A LONDONER'S LIFE *(1916): Sam Cowell £80 in the 1850s; Leotard £180 in the 1860s; Cecilia Loftus and Little Tich £250 in the 1910s; George Robey and R. G. Knowles £200; Yvette Guilbert £300 in the 1890s; Vesta Tilley £350 in the 1900s. Many of those were salaries for exclusive appearances at one hall. It was possible to earn even larger sums, Hibbert*

When Mr. Albert Chevalier had just established himself as a music hall singer in the early nineties, he contentedly worked three 'turns' nightly for thirty six pounds. Shortly he went on a recital tour, and made as much as four hundred and fifty pounds a week . . .

However, it should be remembered that similar or even higher salaries were commanded by other entertainers, eg Adelaine Patti charged £40 per minute for an operatic recital; Henry Irving and Ellen Terry £150 per night each in the 1890s—plus the salaries of their company; David Garrick £100 per night in the 1760s. All would have been reasonable now, even before conversion. Then, as now, a high salary was paid (or said to have been paid) as a form of advertising by the manager concerned, or demanded as a form of barrier by the artist. A combination of both no doubt resulted in George Alexander and Beerbohm Tree receiving £750 a week at the Palace, and Sarah Bernhardt £1000 at the Coliseum in 1913.

In addition to the stars the work force engaged in ancillary services was not inconsiderable (see p 40, and column 3 in the table on p 99). Arthur Sherwell commented on this in LIFE IN WEST LONDON *(2nd ed 1897)*

Included in this innumerable army are hotel, theatrical, and music-hall employees . . . cab 'touts' . . . sandwichmen (for whom the numerous theatres, music-halls, art galleries, exhibitions etc. of the West End provide ready but miserable employment).

Music Hall Companies

Although the Alhambra was the first 'music hall' to be registered as a limited company—3 November 1865—it was not then either a genuine music hall or variety theatre. The London Pavilion was a hall when the London Pavilion Limited was registered on 15 November 1886 with a capital of £180,000 in £5 shares. This was the second London Pavilion, opened in 1885 to replace the first built in 1861 for £12,000 and sold to the

51 *Salary list from the Gaiety, Edinburgh 1890, Edward Moss's first hall. Note that in the case of minor performers one night's salary was held back until after the Saturday night performance—column 1. From* W. H. Boardman's Vaudeville Days

Metropolitan Board of Works in 1878 for £109,347 so that it could be demolished and the environs of Piccadilly improved. The Pavilion's first dividend was 14 per cent. A peak of 16 per cent was reached in 1891 and 1892, before a steady decline set in until 1913 when the dividend was only 2½ per cent. The war saw a gradual improvement in business until by 1920 the dividend almost exactly equalled the average of all payments over the preceding thirty-five years—8½ per cent. The Select Committee on Theatres and Places of Entertainment REPORT *(1892) contains a long interview in which Henry Newsom-Smith—the City accountant who was the first to see music hall purely in terms of high*

STAR PALACE OF VARIETIES.

ABBEY STREET, BERMONDSEY,

LONDON, S.E.

TELEPHONE 1048 HOP.

Augt 17. 1885

7.30	Overture		
7.40	Rodney Folglaze	1. 10. 0
7.50	Miss V. Friend	1. 5. 0
8.5	Tom Leamore	15. 0
8.20	Marie Lloyd	15. 0
8.35	Dectoria	2. 10. 0
8.50	Ray Dwight Ray	5. 0. 0
9.10	Sam Redfern	4. 0. 0
INTERVAL 9.25		
9.30	Bella Bastall	1. 10. 0
9.45	Jas. Castant	2. 10. 0
10.0	The Surles	} 4. 10. 0
10.10	Mass Vincent	}
10.25	Keegan & Elvin	3. 0. 0
10.55	Arthur West	2. 0. 0
11.5	Extra Turn Sal	10. 0
		£ 29 15 0

Income	(1)	(2)	(3)	(4)
	£			£
doors £41,945. 2.8		72	190	
bars £16,039.19.7				
£57,985. 2.3	90,000			524.9.0

Summary of all returns:

ENGLAND:—

1. London (16)	650,000	926	1,181	4,566.0.8
2. Provinces (38)	776,200	1,006	1,410	5,334.0.0
IRELAND (2)	22,000	31	53	252.0.0
SCOTLAND (1)	2,500			100.0.0
	1,450,700			10,252.0.0

Actual music-hall balance sheets are elusive documents especially before an amendment to the Companies Act made it compulsory to append a balance sheet of one sort or another to the annual return of share-holdings. Although in some respects it is not entirely representative (especially by 1915) this Alhambra return (now in the Public Record Office) does indicate the type and proportion of the various expenses incurred in running a variety theatre of the period. In 1916 the Alhambra paid a 10 per cent dividend to its shareholders.

finance—gave evidence in some detail. Unfortunately the Pavilion was not included in an appendix to the Report showing (1) the capital, (2) the number of artistes, (3) the number of employees, (4) salary and wages, (but not other expenditure eg cost of scenery, beer and food, maintenance, gas and electricity) of a selection of halls in London and the provinces. But the figures for the Canterbury and Paragon combined for the year ending 31 January 1892 were given

THE ALHAMBRA COMPANY, LIMITED
BALANCE SHEET, 31 December, 1915

Dr   **Cr**

	£	s	d		£	s	d
To Share Capital:—				By Debtors	1,001	10	5
Authorised—				By Cash at Bankers and in hand	2,646	6	1
100,000 Shares of £1 each £100,000				By Investments:—at cost less writings down			
Issued—				£10,000 4½ per cent. War Loan 1925/1945, valued at £9,673 18 6			
60,000 Shares of £1 each, fully paid	60,000	0	0	£1,700 Alhambra 5 per cent. Debenture Stock (1908), at cost 1,627 14 9			
To Debenture Bonds and Stocks:—				£400 Alhambra 5 per cent, Mortgage Debenture Bonds, at cost 380 0 0			
5% Mortgage Debenture Bonds (Balance) £11,100 0 0					11,681	13	3
4% Debenture Stock 28,930 0 0				By Stock-in-Trade at cost	1,984	15	0
5% Debenture Stock (1908) 15,000 0 0				By Freehold Land, Building, &c.:—			
5% Debenture Stock (1912) 30,000 0 0	85,030	0	0	Alhambra Theatre, at cost less writings down as per last Account 124,697 16 2			
To Sundry Creditors 4,634 18 2				Freehold Property at Walworth, as per last Account 4,962 9 7			
To Interest accrued on Debenture Debt 1,660 10 11	6,295	9	1		129,660	5	9
To Revenue Account:—				By Alterations, Additions and Improvements, as per last Account at cost less writings down £9,000 0 0			
Net Reveue for the year 1915 592 6 7				Less Appropriation of— Reserve A/c £2,000			
Balance from last Account 663 6 3	1,255	12	10	Renewals			

	£	s	d		£	s	d
				Reserve A/c £4,000			
					6,000	0	0
					3,000	0	0
				By Cost of Issue of and Discount upon			
				Five per cent. Debenture Stock			
To Contingency:—				(1912), balance	2,300	0	0
Liability for Excess Profits Duty				By Insurance paid in advance	306	11	5
	£152,581	1	11		£152,581	1	11

REVENUE ACCOUNT for the YEAR ending 31 DECEMBER, 1915

Dr   **Cr**

	£	s	d		£	s	d
To Entertainment Expenses	58,429	15	0	By Entertainment and other Receipts	98,762	15	1
To Management, Front of House and				By Transfer Fees	6	16	0
General Expenses	11,369	10	6	By Interest and Discounts	592	10	4
To Refreshment Expenses	7,368	3	2				
To Advertising	6,852	15	0				
To Lighting and Heating	2,447	2	11				
To Taxes and Water	2,819	14	6				
To Insurance	1,261	18	5				
To Insurance Act Contributions	96	18	3				
To Renewals and Repairs	1,711	7	6				
To Rent Charge	58	15	4				
To Directors' Fees	596	3	11				
To Debenture Trustees' Fees, &c.	247	0	0				
To Audit Fee	100	0	0				
To Legal Expenses	377	16	4				
To Loss on Tours	111	0	10				
To Balance carried to Net Revenue							
Account	5,513	19	9				
	£99,362	1	5		£99,362	1	5

NET REVENUE ACCOUNT for the YEAR ending 31 December, 1915

Dr   **Cr**

	£	s	d		£	s	d
To Interest on Debentures and Debenture Stocks	3,999	14	0	By Balance from Revenue Account	5,513	19	9
To Written off the cost of Issue of and Discount upon 5 per cent. Debenture Stock (1912)	570	12	8				
To Written off Investments	351	6	6				
To Balance carried down	592	6	7				
	£5,513	19	9		£5,513	19	9
				By Balance brought down	592	6	7
				By Balance from last Account	663	6	3
					£1,255	12	10

The Alhambra opened in 1854 as the Royal Panoptican of Science and Art was converted into a music hall in 1860. In a table compiled for the Report of the Select Committee on Theatrical Licences and Regulations (1866) it headed the list of the estimated cost of

LONDON CONCERT HALLS, MUSIC HALLS, AND ENTERTAINMENT GALLERIES

The London music halls, concert halls, &c. the earliest of which was built in 1851, and the latest in 1864, have their value very fairly, though roughly, estimated in the above table, from which a number of small tavern concert rooms are excluded. Some halls may be overrated and some underrated in this table: for example, the Alhambra is put down at 50,000l., although it cost 100,000l., because the smaller sum more nearly represents its value, but the totals are tolerably correct for an estimate.

The music halls, concert halls, &c., in the country that have sprung into existence since the passing of the Act of 1843, may be estimated as bearing the same proportion to the country theatres as the London halls do to the London theatres, viz, nearly two to one. The capital invested in them cannot be far short of a million sterling, and they provide nightly accommodation for at least half a million persons.

	Cost of Buildings and Fittings £	Number of Persons Accommodated Daily
Crystal Palace	1,000,000	100,000
Agricultural Hall	50,000	20,000
St James's Hall	50,000	5,000
St Martin's Hall	50,000	4,000
Exeter Hall	50,000	6,000

Gallery of Illustration	5,000	500
Egyptian Hall	5,000	500
Polygraphic Hall	5,000	500
Polytechnic	20,000	1,000
Alhambra, Leicester-square	50,000	5,000
Oxford, Oxford-street	40,000	2,000
Strand, Strand	30,000	1,500
Canterbury Hall, Lambeth	25,000	1,500
Metropolitan, Edgware-road	25,000	2,000
Regent, Westminster	25,000	1,500
Wilton's, Wellclose-square	20,000	1,500
Evans's, Covent Garden	20,000	1,000
Weston's, Holborn	20,000	1,500
Philharmonic, Islington	20,000	1,500
Highbury Barn, Highbury	20,000	2,000
Cambridge, Shoreditch	16,000	2,000
Winchester, Southwark	15,000	2,000
Lord Raglan, Theobald's-road	12,000	1,500
Middlesex, Drury-lane	12,000	1,200
London Pavilion, Coventry-street	12,000	2,000
South London, London-road	8,000	1,200
Marylebone	8,000	800
Oriental, Poplar	7,000	800
Borough	6,000	1,000
Bedford, Camden Town	5,000	800
Deacon's, Clerkenwell	5,000	800
Trevor, Knightsbridge	5,000	800
Sun, Knightsbridge	5,000	800
Lansdowne, Islington	4,000	600
Rodney, Whitechapel	3,000	600
Apollo, Bethnal-green	3,000	600
Westminster, Pimlico	3,000	800
Nag's Head, Lambeth	2,000	500
Woodman, Hoxton	2,000	500
Eastern Alhambra	2,000	1,000
Swallow-Street	2,000	500
Total, 41 Places	£ 1,667,000	179,300

Most shares in music-hall companies were owned by interested parties, as, to those seeking purely financial reward, the halls did not represent quite as good an investment as could be obtained elsewhere by selective stock buying. In addition the very great fluctuations in the dividends paid by each company (eg The Empire's dividend was 70 per cent in 1896 and 1897, 56 per cent in 1899 and 1900, 5 per cent in 1905, 20 per cent from 1908-13, but nothing in 1914) emphasises both the risky nature of the enterprises and, very markedly, how the steam began to go out of them at the turn of the century, when the average dividends fell sharply below those paid in the late 1880s and early 1890s. This did not, however, prevent some apparently ultra-respectable investors gambling in music-hall shares—usually with a small number only. Thus in 1893 of the 373 shareholders in The Alhambra, 55 gave their occupation as 'married woman' or 'widow' and 30 as 'spinster'. Local halls often attracted the support of local tradesmen, for example shares in Weston's Music Hall Company Limited (formed in 1886 to acquire the Royal Music Hall, Holborn) were held by a barman, admiralty clerk, warehouseman, grocer, tailor, butler, stationmaster, gardener and an assistant librarian at the British Museum in addition to the usual gentlemen, lawyers, comedians and publicans. The company went into liquidation in 1891. In 1892 John Hollingshead took over, renamed it the Royal Holborn Theatre of Varieties. In 1906 it was rebuilt, and in 1925 it was registered at the Holborn Empire Limited. In 1947 it was officially licensed to Moss Empires Ltd by the LCC even though by then it was only a gutted shell following a bombing raid in 1941. Moss Empires was the first of the real big syndicates to be formed around 1900 to combat a slump in music-hall business. Thomas Skinner: STOCK EXCHANGE YEAR BOOK FOR 1901

Directors: H. E. Moss (Chairman), F. Allen, O. Stoll and R. Thornton . . . The Company was registered December 15, 1899 to acquire the proper-

TELEPHONE HORNSEY 2240.
TELEGRAMS—"HONRI, LONDON."

Percy Honri

OFFICES AND STORES·
ALEXANDRA PALACE.
LONDON, N.

PLEASE REPLY

E M P I R E   C R O Y D O N.

WEEK ENDING MAY 1st 1915.

		GROSS RECEIPTS			COST OF COMP⁸ TAKEN OVER.			
Apl 26th	Monday	97	10	4	Clarice Mayne & That	65	.	.
" 27th	Tuesday	111	18	6	Minne Black & Co	20	.	-
" 28th	Wenesday	152	17	6	Gregie	6	.	.
" 29th	Thursday	125	10	9	Sisters Julian	8	.	.
" 30th	Friday	114	12	-	Pictures	5	2	6
May 1st	Saturday	204	9	3		£104	2	6
	Less to Hause	806	13	0				
					Share @ 50%			
		£ 606	18	9		£303	0	5

Cash

$£ 5$ Notes = £225 - 0 - 0

Gold = 78 - 0 - 0

Silver = 9 - 0

Copper = 0

£ 303 · 9 · 0

53 *The weekly balance sheet for Percy Honri's '1915*
Revue'—promotion for which included a full front page
advertisement in The Daily Mail *2 August 1915*

54 *Token for Benjamin Lang's Victoria Musical Gallery, Manchester. Lang was listed as a 'Beer Retailer' in the Manchester directories for 1840 and 1845. But in 1850 and 1852, he is listed as 'Beer Retailer and Concert Room'. There is nothing intrinsically unique about the use of tokens in music halls. They were merely a late survival of the trade token*

ties and business of the following companies:— Birmingham Empire Palace, Ltd.; Cardiff, Newport and Swansea Empire Palace, Ltd.; Edinburgh Empire Palace, Ltd.; Glasgow Empire Palace, Ltd.; Liverpool, Leeds and Hull Empire Palaces Ltd.; London District Empire Palaces, Ltd.; London Hippodrome, Ltd.; Newcastle Empire Palace, Ltd.; Nottingham Empire Palace, Ltd.; and Sheffield Empire Palace, Ltd. . . . The authorised capital is £1,000,000 in shares of £5, half being 5% cumulative preference, and half ordinary, and power was taken to issue 4% perpetual debenture stock for £400,000. Of the preference capital £470,705, of the ordinary £425,765, and of the debenture stock £273,135 have been subscribed and paid up . . .

London District Empire Palaces Limited owned

Empires at Finsbury Park, New Cross, Stratford, and Holloway. By 1912 the Bradford Empire, Liverpool Olympia, Glasgow Coliseum, Glasgow and Birmingham Grands, and the Summerhill Palace, Birmingham, had been added to the chain. THE STOCK EXCHANGE YEAR BOOK FOR 1924 *recorded that*

in 1921 an arrangement was arrived at with the London Theatres of Variety Limited, and the Variety Theatres Controlling Company, Ltd. for co-operation . . .

LONDON THEATRES OF VARIETY LIMITED

Directors: Sir F. Eley (Chairman), Sir A. C. Peake, Sir G. Dance, C. Gulliver (Managing Director), R. B. Stephens, W. S. Gordon Michie, W. Payne, O.B.E., J. Davis, R. H. Gillespie, H. J. Gulliver . . . registered March 2, 1908 . . . owns or leases nineteen theatres of variety in London and the suburbs; controls Variety Theatres Controlling Company Limited, Capital Syndicate Ltd., Hammersmith Palace of Variety Ltd., Holborn Empire Ltd., Empire Palace (Woolwich) Ltd., Empire Palace (Poplar) Ltd., New Camberwell Palace, Ltd., Camberwell Production Ltd., Productions (Richmond) Ltd., and Croydon Hippodrome Ltd.

This 'arrangement' was the prelude to further post-1923 remarshalling of resources to combat changing social conditions, decreasing audiences, and competition from the wireless and, of course, films. It was no accident that London Theatres of Variety went bankrupt in 1928, while Moss Empires with its greater array of theatres and connections continued to prosper.

LIST OF SOURCES

CHAPTER ONE

Geoffrey Chaucer   *The Canterbury Tales* (c1387)
                       modern version by Neville Coghill (1951)
T. Cromwell   *History and Description of Clerkenwell* (1828)
Benjamin Disraeli   *Sybil or The Two Nations* (1845)
Erasmus   *Praise of Folly* (1509) translated by Betty Radice (1971)
The Hon F.L.G.   *The Swell's Night Guide Through the Metropolis* (c1840)
Thomas Frost   *The Old Showmen and the Old London Fairs* (1874)
Sir John Hawkins   *A General History of the Science and Practice of Music* (1776)
J. W. Hudson   *The History of Adult Education* (1851)
Blanchard Jerrold   *London* (1872, repr 1971)
Peter Kalm   *Kalm's Account of His Visit to England on His Way to America in 1748* (1753) translated by Joseph Lucas (1892)
William Cook Taylor   *Tour in the Manufacturing Districts of Lancashire* (2nd ed 1842)
Ned Ward   *The London Spy Compleat* (1704)
                       Walk to Islington with a Description of New Tunbridge Wells and Sadler's Musick-House (1699)
Edmund Yates   *His Recollections and Experiences*, Vol I (1884)

CHAPTER TWO

Art Journal (April 1856)
The Builder (1858, 1890, 1893)
Building News (1859, 1861, 1868)

	The Era (1872, 1873)
Stephen Gosson	*Plays Confuted* (1590)
H. G. Hibbert	*Fifty Years of a Londoner's Life* (1916)
T. Middlebrook	Letter to Raymond Mander & Joe Mitchenson
	Minutes of the Committee of the Council on Education Reports by Her Majesty's Inspector of Schools 1852-3, volume II, General Report . . . for 1852 (1853)
	National Review (1861)
	New York Statesman (1826)
	Saturday Review (1887)
	Report of Select Committee on Public Houses (1854)
	Report of Select Committee on Theatrical Licences and Regulations (1866)
	Report of Select Committee on the Metropolitan Fire Brigade (1876)
Charles Weldon	*Reminiscences of Music Hall and Variety Entertainments, Manchester 1864-6* (2nd ed 1907)

CHAPTER THREE

	Daily Telegraph (1894, 1907)
Mrs Ormiston Chant	*Why We Attacked the Empire* (1895)
P. Anderson Graham	*The Rural Exodus* (1892)
	Northampton Independent (1911)
	Pall Mall Gazette (1894)
H. G. Hibbert	*Fifty Years of a Londoner's Life* (1916)
	The Star (1894)
	The Times (1912)

CHAPTER FOUR

H. O. Brunn	*The Story of the Original Dixieland Jazz Band* (1961)
Percy Burton	'How a Variety Theatre Is Run', *Strand Magazine*, May 1907
Edward Gordon Craig	'The Vitality of Music Hall', *The Mask* (1912)
Benjamin Disraeli	*Sybil or The two Nations* (1845)
	The Era (1919)
A. G. Gardiner	*Pillars of Society* (1914)
Charles E. Hands	'A Common Person's Complaint', *Daily Mail* (1913)
Christopher Hassall	*Rupert Brooke* (1964)
Keith, MacAllister	*Blue Book* (1920)
Geoffrey Keynes (ed)	*The Letters of Rupert Brooke* (1968)
	Report of National Council of Public Morals. Cinema Commission of Inquiry (1917)
Siegfried Sassoon	'Blighters', *Collected Poems* (1961)
	Town Topics (12 April 1919)

CHAPTER FIVE

James Agate	*Immoment Toys* (1945)
Max Beerbohm	'Yvette Guilbert and Albert Chevalier', *Saturday Review* (23 June 1892)
Albert Chevalier	'The Coster in Society', *The Graphic* (1892)
	Daily Mail (1913, 1922)
	Daily Telegraph (1922)
Newman Flower (ed)	*The Journals of Arnold Bennett 1896-1910* (1932)
W. L. George	*London Mosaic* (1921)
Roger Lancelyn Green (ed)	*The Diaries of Lewis Carroll* (1953)
H. G. Hibbert	*Fifty Years of a Londoner's Life* (1916)
Holbrook Jackson	*The Eighteen Nineties*
Dame Laura Knight	*Oil Paint and Grease Paint* (1936)
Harry Lauder	Letter to J. Howie Milligan (8 April 1910)
James L. Limbacher	*Four Aspects of the Film* (1968)
Marie Lloyd	'Miss Marie Lloyd criticizes her own risqué songs', *New York Telegraph* (1897)
Rachel Low and Roger Manvell	*The History of the British Film 1896-1906* (1948)
Paul Nash	*Outline* (1949)
A. J. Park and Charles Douglas Stuart (eds)	*Variety Stars* (1895)
James Ritchie	*Days and Nights in London* (1880)
Frank Rutter	*Since I was 25* (1927)
	The Sketch (1895)
	The Star (1892, 1893)
George Alexander Stevens	*The Adventures of a Speculist* (1788)
	The Times (1904)
W. R. Titterton	*From Theatre to Music Hall* (1912)

CHAPTER SIX

Max Beerbohm	'At the Tivoli', *Saturday Review* (1898). 'In a Music Hall', *Saturday Review* (1901). 'Music Halls of My Youth', *The Listener* (1943)
Charles Booth	*Life and Labour of the London Poor, 3rd Series, Religious Influences, Vol 3: The City of London and the West End* (1902)
	Church Reformer (June 1892)
Richard Doyle	*Bird's Eye Views of Society* (1864)
Robert Emmons	*The Life and Opinions of Walter Richard Sickert* (1941)
Newman Flower (ed)	*The Journals of Arnold Bennett 1896-1910 and 1911-1921* (1932)
George Gamble	*The 'Halls* (1899)

W. L. George	*London Mosaic* (1921)
The Rev H. R. Haweis	*Music and Morals* (1871)
Rudyard Kipling	*Something of Myself* (1937)
Mass Observation	*The Pub and the People* (1943, repr 1970)
[Henry Mayhew ?]	*Labour and the Poor: The Manufacturing Districts . . .* Letter VII, *Morning Chronicle* (1849)
George Moore	*Confessions of a Young Man* (1886)
John Osborne	*The Entertainer* (1957)
	Report of Select Committee on Theatrical Licences and Regulations (1866)
George Bernard Shaw	*The World* (1894)
Arthur Symons	*Cities and Sea Coasts and Islands* (1919)
	'Prologue: In the Stalls', *London Nights* (1895)
	Tempted London: Young Men (1888)
Raymond Williams	*The Long Revolution* (1961)
Thomas Wright	*Some Habits and Customs of the Working Class by a Journeyman Engineer* (1867)

CHAPTER SEVEN

	Daily Mail (1913)
T. H. S. Escott	*England Its People, Policy and Pursuits* (1870)
Newman Flower (ed)	*The Journals of Arnold Bennett 1896-1910* (1932)
W. N. M. Geary	*The Law of Theatres and Music-Halls* (1885)
Henry Arthur Jones	*An Open Letter to the Right Honourable Winston Churchill, MP* (1910)
John Palmer	*The Future of the Theatre* (1913)
	Report of Select Committee on Theatres and Places of Entertainment (1892)
	Report of Select Committee on Theatrical Licences and Regulations (1866)
George Bernard Shaw	'The Shewing-up of Blanco Posnet': Preface (1909) in *Complete Prefaces of Bernard Shaw* (1965)

CHAPTER EIGHT

The Alhambra Company Limited	Balance Sheet 31 December 1915
H. G. Hibbert	*Fifty Years of a Londoner's Life* (1916)
	'Music-Hall Business', *St James Gazette* (27 April 1892)
	Report of Select Committee on Theatrical Licences and Regulations (1866)
	Report of Select Committee on Theatres and Places of Entertainment (1892)
Arthur Sherwell	*Life in West London* (2nd ed 1897)
Thomas Skinner	*Stock Exchange Year Book 1901*
	Stock Exchange Year Book 1924

ACKNOWLEDGEMENTS

I am most grateful for permission to reproduce illustrations of material in the possession of: Birmingham Public Library, 4, 5; British Broadcasting Corporation, 26; British Museum, 6, 18, 30, 34, 40, 46, 49; British Music Hall Society, 10; Barry Brown, 39; Central Press Photos Ltd, 24; David and Jill Cox, 17, 45; Edward Craig, 9, 11, 15; Greater London Council, Architect's Department, 86; Guildhall Library, 2, 8a, 47; Peter Honri, 53; Islington Public Libraries, Finsbury Local Collection, 3; London Museum, 28; Raymond Mander and Joe Mitchenson, 13, 14, 27, 41, 48; The Mansell Collection, 1, 29; Northampton Public Library, 21; *Punch*, 22; Radio Times Hulton Picture Library, 23, 35, 36, 38; David Samuelson, 50; The Survey of London, 16; Tulane University Library, Archive of New Orleans Jazz, 25; Victoria and Albert Museum, Enthoven Collection, 7, 12, 31, 37, 42, 43, 44.

The other illustrations are from the author's collection.

I must thank Clive Bingley, John Cavenagh, Edward Craig, Diana Howard (particularly for compiling London Theatres & Music Halls 1850-1950), Raymond Mander and Joe Mitchenson, and Brian Rust for information readily given. I am, of course, fully responsible for the use made of their suggestions. The following institutions provided invaluable assistance: Birmingham Public Libraries—Local History Collection; British Broadcasting Corporation—Written Archives Centre (Mary S. Hodgson); British Film Institute—Book Library; The British Museum Library; The Guildhall Library (Ralph Hyde); Haringay Public Libraries—Hornsey and Muswell Hill Branches; Jesus College, Cambridge—Archives (Mrs P. R. Jones); The London Library; Manchester Public Libraries—Local History Collection; The Marconi Company (Mrs B. Hance); New York Public Library; Northampton Public Library; The Royal Institute of British Architects Library; Tulane University Library—Archive of New Orleans Jazz (Richard B. Allen); University of London—Institute of Education Library; The Victoria and Albert Museum—Enthoven Collection (Tony Latham); Yale University Library (Sandra Whiteley). I must thank the following for allowing me to reproduce non-photographic material in their collections: The Public Record Office; The Trustees of the British Museum; The Trustees of the Victoria and Albert Museum; and the Editors of *The Daily Telegraph* and *Daily Mail*.

Permission to use copyright material is gratefully acknowledged to the following:

George Allen & Unwin Ltd — Rachel Low and Roger Manvell, *The History of the British Film 1896-1906*

Mrs George Bambridge, Macmillan & Co Ltd, The Macmillan Co of Canada Ltd and Doubleday & Co Ltd — Rudyard Kipling, *Something of Myself*

Butterworth & Co (Publishers) Ltd — G. E. C. Catlin, *Liquor Control*

G. Bell & Sons Ltd — John Palmer, *The Future of the Theatre*

Brussel & Brussel — James L. Limbacher, *Four Aspects of Film*

Cassell & Co Ltd and A. P. Watt & Son — Roger Lancelyn Green (ed), *The Diaries of Lewis Carroll*

Cassell & Co Ltd — Newman Flower (ed), *The Journals of Arnold Bennett*

Chatto & Windus and the author — Raymond Williams, *The Long Revolution*

William Collins & Sons Ltd — W. L. George, *London Mosaic*; Arthur Symons, *Cities and Sea-coasts and Islands*

Constable & Co Ltd — Frank Rutter, *Since I was 25*

H. E. G. Craig — Edward Gordon Craig, *The Vitality of Music Hall*

J. M. Dent — A. G. Gardiner, *Pillars of Society*

Faber & Faber Ltd — Robert Emmons, *The Life and Opinions of Walter Richard Sickert*; Geoffrey Keynes (ed), *The Letters of Rupert Brooke*; Paul Nash, *Outline*

Faber & Faber Ltd and Harcourt, Brace, Jovanovich — Christopher Hassall, *Rupert Brooke*

Garnstone Press — H. G. Hibbert, *Fifty Years of a Londoner's Life*

David Higham Associates — John Osborne, *The Entertainer*

Jarrolds Publishers (London) Ltd — W. H. Boardman, *Vaudeville Days*

Methuen & Co Ltd — P. Anderson Graham, *The Rural Exodus*

Penguin Books Ltd — Geoffrey Chaucer, *The Canterbury Tales*; Erasmus, *Praise of Folly*

Rupert Hart-Davis — Max Beerbohm, 'At the Tivoli'; 'In a Music Hall'; Music Halls of My Youth'; 'Yvette Guilbert and Albert Chevalier'

G. T. Sassoon — Siegfried Sassoon, 'Blighters'

Seven Dials Press — Mass Observation, *The Pub and the People*

The Society of Authors as the literary representative of the Estate of Holbrook Jackson — Holbrook Jackson, *The Eighteen-Nineties*

The Society of Authors on behalf of the Bernard Shaw Estate — George Bernard Shaw: 'The Shewing-up of Blanco Posnet'—the preface

The Stock Exchange Year Book

112